DREAM IT

SIX PRINCIPLES FOR AN AWESOME LIFE

LIVE IT

SHANE PERRY, SR.

DREAM IT

SIX PRINCIPLES FOR AN AWESOME LIFE

LIVE IT

w

WHITAKER
HOUSE

DREAM IT, LIVE IT:
Six Principles for an Awesome Life

www.drshaneperry.com

ISBN: 978-1-62911-980-9
eBook ISBN: 978-1-62911-981-6
Printed in the United States of America
© 2017 by Shane Perry Sr.

Whitaker House
1030 Hunt Valley Circle
New Kensington, PA 15068
www.whitakerhouse.com

Library of Congress Cataloging-in-Publication Data (Pending)

1 2 3 4 5 6 7 8 9 10 11 ⨆ 24 23 22 21 20 19 18 17

CONTENTS

PROLOGUE

PROLOGUE

As I sit here after my daily time of prayer, I am trying to visualize you in my mind. That's right, I want to see who I'm writing this book for. This is important for me because I believe that I know the type of person that you are. Anyone who would buy this kind of book has a similar view about life as I do. You have a feeling that there must be more to life than what you are experiencing right now. Yes, I feel like I know you and I am connected to you because I too have been where you are.

I also have this internal drive that won't allow me to settle for a mundane and goalless life. I have seen too many people live lives of fulfillment, happiness, and success for me to think that you or I are excluded from this group. I have read about people overcoming seemingly impossible circumstances; I've seen with my own eyes people who are living their best lives ever. The thing I realized, and something I want to stress to you at the beginning of this book, is that those people are not special or separate from you and me. They are, in fact, just like us, with only one difference: *they dared to capture a vision in their minds and hold it there until it became a reality.*

I have followed the six principles that I lay out for you in this book. They have worked for me, time and time again. They are timeless truths, rooted in the pages of Scripture, and they carry great validity when followed and applied. We were all put here for a purpose and we each have been given the tools to follow that purpose through using the six principles in this book. We can, as the title suggests, live an awesome life. This life is possible when we receive a revelation of who we are and what we are here to do in this life, and when we formulate a vison that charts the course to get us there.

In this book you will hear my personal testimony of the times when these principles have worked in my life and how they will work for you as well. You will be encouraged by my firsthand accounts of the amazing things God has done in my life after discovering these principles and making them a part of my everyday practice. You will be inspired to put your confidence in God's ability to transform you through the power of writing, speaking, and acting upon your God-given vision. I will show you how to banish doubts and fears that try to talk you out of your vision before you even get started. You will find that doubt is actually a good thing in the beginning because it is the first stage to stretching your mind beyond your current limitations.

We will explore the sheer power of simply writing down what you want to happen in your life. This is such a life-changing moment for so many people because it's the place where your future comes into focus as you begin to picture the possibilities of what can happen when you allow yourself to let go and dream while you are awake. This is a truly moving part of the vision process because you start to imagine possibilities where there were once limitations. You will learn to visualize yourself in the future and see what you could become instead of being stuck where you are for the rest of your life. This is perhaps the best way to describe this part of the vision process. It's the only true way to become unstuck from the cycles that have governed your experience up to this point. You will learn exactly what you need to ask yourself to set up a framework by which to live the rest of your life.

> **This is perhaps the best way to describe this part of the vision process. It's the only true way to become unstuck from the cycles that have governed your experience up to this point.**

We will also discover an incredibly effective way in which we can become intimate with our vison by speaking it every day. Proverbs 18:21 says that, *"Death and life are in the power of the tongue: and they that love it shall eat the fruit thereof."* You always have a choice when you speak. You can either speak death or life in any given situation. I have found that speaking life doesn't come easily or automatically to any of us. The reason for this is because we have been raised in an environment of negativity in a world that likes to express impossibilities instead of possibilities. It therefore takes effort on our part to learn how to speak life.

I will show you that through the repetition that comes from focusing on what you *do* want instead of what you *don't* want, your speech will become more intentional. This focused talk will cause you to speak life and literally fall in love with this way of speaking. *"They that love it will eat the fruit thereof."* You will eat the fruit of the words you speak, nothing more and nothing less. So you have a choice: speak life or death. I want to teach you the principles that rule our speech and how to become a person that speaks your vision into existence.

> **There has to be a place in your vision-writing process where you draw a line from where you are to where you want to be.**

I have found that although some people have learned how to write out a vision and also how to speak about the things they want, they still find that they don't see what they have visualized manifesting in the material world. This is due to the fact that just seeing and speaking alone will not give you the desires of your heart. There has to be a place in your vision-writing process where you draw a line from where you are to where you want to be. This is where the next portion of our study will lead us. In this section we will discover the principle of planning for the success of our vision. I have found that when we plan for the success of our vision, we are giving ourselves something to work with. This becomes the strategy that gives us a charted course for our future destiny. I will show you how to write out a plan for each of your goals and how to break them down into manageable parts so you can immediately go to work on what you believe.

The last principle we will discover is how to become a person of action. There is always a *doing* that accompanies *believing*. Many times, we are left with a pipedream simply because we either don't know what to do or because we refuse to do anything. When our faith is not accompanied with action, then we are simply sending up weak prayers. It's only when we follow through on our vision with action that we will start to see progress. I have found that there is always something we can do to activate our vision, and the sooner we get started, the better. You will discover that there are immediate steps you can take regardless of where you are in life or what time of the day you decide to take action. There is always an email that can be sent, junk food to be thrown out, a run you can go on, or a phone call you can make. Action becomes your greatest ally in seeing the fulfillment of your vision. I can't wait to see you take action because incredible things open to you when you follow this principle.

As we move through the six principles of living your vision, I want you to open your mind to the possibilities of what can happen if you put them into action. If you are tired of living below your potential and seek a richer, purposeful, and more rewarding life, then you have the right book in your hands. Together we will learn how to become all that God has for us to be in life. You *can* live a life of fulfillment and joy. Within these pages you will find the keys to obtaining your vision and you will truly learn how to dream it and live it!

INTRODUCTION

INTRODUCTION:
IT WORKED FOR ME

I will never forget that cold Alabama morning at my mother-in-law's house. There I was lying on her floor trying to figure out how I had found myself in the predicament I was in. I felt so weak and helpless as I tried to figure out what my next move was. I had lost my apartment in California and was completely broke; all of my possessions in storage were about to be auctioned off for lack of payment. Not to mention the fact that one of my vehicles was being repossessed and the other was about to be towed in California. My wife was pregnant with our first child and I had no job and seemingly no future prospects for change.

Stretched out, flat on my face, I asked God a question: "Lord, I know nothing is wrong with You, so what's wrong with me?" I will never forget the answer that came back. God spoke to me so clearly, saying, "You have lost your dream."

I knew exactly what He meant by this statement. You see, when I was nineteen years old, I attended the Holy Convocation of the Church of God in Christ in Memphis, Tennessee. This large convention had been going on for over one hundred years, with thousands of people in attendance every year. I remember sitting in the nosebleed section of the Cook Convention Center where the meeting was being held, hearing the voice of the Lord speaking to my spirit. He said to me, "One day you will stand on that stage and preach."

> There is always a magnetic force that attracts all you need and desire when you get back to your vision.

Now, back on my mother-in-law's floor, God reminded me of that moment. He told me that I had to get my vision back in this area and that now was the time to start. It's amazing to think that I needed so much at this time in my life and that God was telling me to start with a dream. There is always a magnetic force that attracts all you need and desire when you get back to your vision. What I thought I needed was wrapped up in my ability to peer into the future and go after all that God was calling me to be.

Back on that floor, I let myself dream again. Not only did I have my vision restored for what God spoke to me on that November night in Memphis, but I started dreaming about every other aspect of my life as well. I took out some paper, grabbed a pen, and began to write. It was an amazing experience, because I knew that I was free to dream whatever I desired to see happen. I declared that one day I would preach in the Holy Convocation, because that was where God had instructed me to go first. Then I felt received visions for every aspect of my life.

> **Take off all the constraints concerning the things that have held you back from your destiny.**
> **Allow yourself, as I did, to dream the highest and most outlandish dream that you can imagine.**

As I pondered all these things, I decided right then and there not to limit my vision. I knew that if I was going to dream, I should make it big. So there I was, fresh out of homelessness and living with my mother-in-law, and yet I wrote out what my dream house would look like. There was a place there called Over the Mountain, where all of the wealthy people in Birmingham lived. So I wrote down in my first vision that I wanted to live in a million-dollar home in Over the Mountain. I refused to put a limit on what I believed God could do for me in my life. This is what I will challenge you do to as you read this book. Take off all the constraints concerning the things that have held you back from your destiny. Allow yourself, as I did, to dream the highest and most outlandish dream that you can imagine. As I wrote down the words, I recognized that I had some basic needs that were making me feel like my dream should be smaller. Still I persisted and made a firm decision to go for it, all of it.

Something amazing happened when I made this choice to dream, and it began with my greatest need: a place to live. Two weeks after writing out my vision, my wife called me about some affordable houses she had found that we should look into. I had started working at a church and was making enough money that I felt we could get into a cheap house with a low rent. When I called the listing she had found on Craigslist, I seemed to have an instant connection with the man who answered the phone. He was a preacher from California and we had quite a bit in common. After we talked on the phone extensively, he invited me to lunch. At lunch he talked to me about a plan he had for making money in real estate, even in a down market. After lunch he took me to see several of his houses that were in my price range. After looking at them, he asked me where my wife was. I told him that she was at home and He said that we should go get her.

We picked her up and drove up on the mountain. When we got there he showed us a million-dollar house that he had. When we started walking through the house, he continuously asked my wife if she could see certain items of hers in that home. It was amazing to hear him saying this to us, knowing that I had just written out in my vision of where I wanted to live. Here we were walking through the exact type of house in the exact area that I had envisioned! Understand that as we walked through this house, my bank account was overdrawn and I had bad credit. Nevertheless, I had a vision—and vision always trumps limitations of every kind.

After we looked at that house, we all went our separate ways. Later that day, the man called back and asked me to come to his house because he needed to talk to me about something. My wife and I went together and we sat on the other side of the desk from him. I remember it like it was yesterday. Then he said to us, "Yes or no, do you want to live in that house?" I told him that the rent on that house was $15,000 down and $5,000 a month, which I couldn't afford. He replied, "I didn't ask you that. Yes or no, do you *want* to live in that house?" I said I did. Without a word, the man slid a set of keys across the desk. We moved into a million-dollar home that day. What an amazing turn of events! Just two weeks earlier, I was on my mother-in-law's floor wondering what I was going to do and now here I was living the dream I had written down on that piece of paper! I'm not telling you this to brag; I'm telling you this because of the incredible principles that I will share with you in this book—principles that will turn your life completely around. Vision is so powerful—powerful enough that it took me from being homeless to moving into my dream home in the same year.

Over the course of the next couple of years, I saw other things begin to come to pass for me as I pursued my vision. Yes, even the thing that started all of this in the first place. In 2009, I stood on the stage at the Holy Convocation for the Church of God in Christ at the Cook Convention Center in Memphis, Tennessee. The amazing thing was that it was the last time in its 100-plus-year history that it would be held there. It was being moved to St. Louis, Missouri, the following year, where it has been held ever since. If it hadn't happened when it did, it wouldn't ever have been possible for it to happen at all. God's timing is perfect and everything serves a purpose.

It's interesting to note that I preached again in the Convocation in 2010, the first one held in St. Louis. You see, if

I hadn't been evicted from my apartment, then I wouldn't have taken a job at the home church of my youth. If I hadn't taken that job, then I wouldn't have been the in the position to book the speakers for our local conferences. When I was put in that position, I was put in direct contact with the leaders who would eventually open the doors for me to be able to stand on that platform. There was a perfect design in all of it that led me to ultimately seeing my vision come to pass. I want you to know that no matter how things look for you right now, there is a greater design for your future that you may not see yet. Stay motivated and keep your eyes on your vision and you too will see great things happen for you.

No matter how things look for you right now, there is a greater design for your future that you may not see yet. Stay motivated and keep your eyes on your vision and you too will see great things happen for you.

Not only did these things happen, eventually I was launched into full-time ministry and I was able to make a living doing what I love to do, which is full-time speaking. All of this happened because in a moment of desperation, I recaptured my vision, and through that vision I was able to live the life that I envisioned. I want you to experience the ecstasy of being able to live a truly fulfilling life, a life that is one of amazement, adventure, and unfolding blessing.

This life is just as available to you as it was for me. You need only to get a vision of what you want your future to look like and dare to be bold enough to pursue it. Within you is an abundance of untapped potential just waiting to be released. There is no way you can convince me that you were put here to be miserable. No, we were put here to live long, productive lives that have an impact on all those we come into contact with.

I know that deep within you there is a longing for something more meaningful in your life. You may have become complacent and resigned to the fact that you just have to live with the cards you've been dealt. I want you to know that this is infinitely untrue. You serve a great God with great plans for your life, and they are just waiting to unfold. Look at what God thinks about you from this passage in Jeremiah: *"For I know the plans I have for you, declares the* LORD, *plans for welfare and not for evil, to give you a future and a hope"* (29:11 ESV). God has amazing plans for you that He wants to reveal and manifest in your life.

> **You serve a great God with great plans for your life,**
> **and they are just waiting to unfold.**

In the next chapter, we will discuss how to find out what these plans are but for now I want you to focus on the fact that He has a plan for you. You no longer have to live a life of barely getting by, hating your job, and wishing that there was more to life. You don't have to wish; you can know and experience the fact that life is full of hope and that God has an amazing future for you. Open up your heart and your mind to this new truth so that you can live a life of greatness. You can make an impression and impact on the very fabric of our world. We have *all* been called to live on a higher plane, experiencing all the joy that comes from fulfilling our destiny through our vision. *All*—includes you, too. This life of unfolding majesty is just waiting for you to step into it and experience it fully. When you do, you'll find what you've been looking for your whole life.

> **This life of unfolding majesty is just waiting for you to step into it and experience it fully. When you do, you'll find what you've been looking for your whole life.**

Here's the question: What is it that you would really like to do in life? Do you know that all things are possible to the person that believes? If you believe that you can live a more satisfying existence and that you have the faith to write it out in a vision, then you will see it all happen in your life. The power of a vision isn't limited to some elite group of people who have an inside connection to the divine; it is available to all and can be accessed by all. All you have to be willing to do is put your fears aside and go for it. Go for that dream that you once had but you now feel you are too old to pursue. Go for that business you've always wanted to start. Write that book you have always wanted to write. Whatever it is, I want you to know that you can do it. As we progress through this book, you will see exactly how to do this and experience life at the highest levels.

This process has never failed me. Some things like the house manifested quickly, while other things have taken more time. But I have discovered that whenever I have written down my dreams and followed through by walking out the principles of the vision, those dreams have ultimately come to pass for me. Here's another example of vision at work. I remember one faithful day when I wrote down that I would speak for Bishop T. D. Jakes. This was a dream I had for years, and a dream that many other preachers have dreamed. Yet there was something different this time when I decided to write it into my vision. I remember that I wrote it down in February and it came to pass in April of that year and again that June. It was an amazing feeling to go back to that sheet of paper and see that what I had written down actually came to pass. That's the power of the vision-writing process. It gives you a clear path to what you desire, and also the tools to be able to navigate your way to that end.

You can use the principles in this book to see your dreams come to life. There is nothing beyond your reach when you have a God-inspired vision for your life. You have the green light to pursue your goals and watch Him manifest your greatest desires. I want you to know that you can do this. Don't fall for the mindset that this all sounds good and that you're glad it happened to me. No! Dare to believe that it can happen for you. You too can live your destined vision from God's great design. You can have all that is promised to you. You can live a happy, abundant, and fulfilling life. Allow yourself to do what I did and banish your doubts and fears and take a chance on vision. You have nothing to lose here. You can truly be, have, and do what you see in your future. It can and will become a reality if you have the fortitude to step out on this process and see it through to the end.

PRINCIPLE ONE

1

PRINCIPLE ONE:
FINDING GOD'S VISION FOR YOUR LIFE

I have to admit that I feel like I have an advantage when it comes to this area of life. I have always seemed to know what I was supposed to do with my life. It has always been there, even before I was born. Of course a calling is just that—it's God calling you before you ever got to the earth realm. Your purpose is God's unique design for your life, and once discovered, it will forever change the course of your life.

My life began in a very difficult way. My mother was raped and became pregnant with me. I didn't find this out until years later of course, but once I was aware of it, I found myself moved more by my mother's resolve in this matter than with the circumstances of my conception. My mother thought about aborting me, but she heard a voice telling her that I would impact the world one day. I am so glad that she listened to that voice! When I was born my grandmother told my mother that I would someday be a preacher. So you see, this has been with me my entire life. Lest you think that I always acquiesced to this calling, I must admit that I had several years where my life was anything but the life of a preacher. I dealt with alcoholism and other addictive behaviors in my past that sought to derail my future, but even in those times, I had this overwhelming sense that there was more for me, that I had a greater purpose to fulfill.

> **You see, the only true way to happiness in a vocation is to do what calls to you—to do the thing that makes working enjoyable.**

Growing up, I was always fascinated by TV preachers. I know this sounds strange, and I admit that it is, until you see the hand of purpose at work. I was always attracted to what I would ultimately become. The Latin word for *vocation* means "to call" and is an important thing to consider when dealing with your purpose. You see, the only true way to happiness in a vocation is to do what calls to you—to do the thing that makes working enjoyable. As I write this book, I just completed a 55,000-word book yesterday and submitted it to my publisher. This is the second such book I have submitted in two months. This means I have written over 100,000 words in a matter of months, and here I am writing this book the day after completing one of those books. What would compel me to revert back to writing so fast on the third book? It's because writing calls to me. When I write, I feel like the words just flow through me from the spirit realm, from the things I have researched leading up to writing, and also things I have picked up through my twenty-one years of preaching. I love to write on the subject of vision, so this book calls to me and can't wait to be written. As I write for hours, the time feels as if it's just moments, because I love to be right here writing about these principles to you right now.

When I teach, all that I have studied in preparation for the message I am about to deliver pours out of me. Sometimes while I am preaching I find myself amazed and humbled at the things I'm saying because I know that they are coming from a place that has called to me my whole life. This is what it is like to live on purpose, to have a life completely sold out to your divine destiny. This is the life God wants to give you, and you can start to live it right now, in this very moment.

> **You only need to take the next step in front of you and keep walking. God wants to see you live out your life purposefully and in harmony with the great calling He has for you.**

One of Lao-tzu's most famous lines from the *Tao Te Ching* states, "The journey of a thousand miles begins with one step." As you take this ancient advice, you will carry with you the key to starting any venture with God. You only need to take the next step in front of you and keep walking. God wants to see you live out your life purposefully and in harmony with the great calling He has for you.

I realize that this is not the normal experience for most of us as it relates to our purpose. Most likely, you did not have a birthing experience that included witnesses who knew your future calling, as was the case with my grandmother. I know that not everyone grew up in an environment where they could nurture their calling and be exposed to the sort of things I was exposed to. So I know that my experience is unique. That being said, that's no excuse for not seeking out and finding your calling. It doesn't have to be religious in nature. It can involve art, music, cooking, child rearing, athletics, or even accounting. God gives people a wide range of gifts and calls them into a wide range of roles.

That's what I want to share with you in this chapter. I want to give you all you need to find and fulfill your purpose so that you can live a life of oneness with your true calling. You may not be called to be a preacher but you are called to do something of great importance. You were intelligently designed to do something of substance in the world. You were not made to just to make it. You were not put here to live an average existence. You were formed by an almighty God to thrive and excel at what you were created for.

YOUR CONNECTION WITH GOD

The first thing you have to do in order to find the true reason for your existence is establish, or reestablish, your connection with God. There is no magic formula for this. It is only found by setting aside time for seeking God on a daily basis. Every morning I get up at 4:30 a.m. and come down to my study. I take the next two hours before anyone else is awake in my house and I spend time with God. I even do this on weekends and holidays. What's the reason for this? It's because this is a scared time that I set apart to continue to grow my relationship with

God and get instructions on the future of what He has for me. Not everyone has two hours to set aside everyday, so make it one hour or half an hour, or fifteen minutes. But make it a regular appointment . Any time spent with God is better than no time spent with Him. I could wait until the kids leave for school and do this at 9:30 a.m. instead if I wanted to, but I know the importance of seeking God early. Even the psalmist echoes this sentiment in Psalm 63:1: *"Early will I seek You."*

> There is an energy and a power that comes from the presence of God, and when you tap into this eternal power you are energized throughout your day.

I know that you will throw up a whole host of excuses as to why you can't do this. You will say that you don't want to be sleepy all day and struggle to stay awake at work. I can assure you, most of you do this anyway; that's why Starbucks is taking over the world! In all honesty, since I have made this a daily practice, I have had more energy than I have ever had in my life. I don't nap and sometimes it takes me a while to fall asleep when I do lay down, sometime between 9:30 and 10:00 p.m. I also run between three and five miles every day, even after arising so early. The reason is simple—there is an energy and a power that comes from the presence of God, and when you tap into this eternal power you are energized throughout your day. I literally go to bed at night with joy thinking about being able to wake up for my early morning time with God. You may say that you just don't have enough hours in the day and that taking out more time from your sleep will only increase an already long day. I have discovered that since I have made this my daily practice, I am so much more productive than at any other time in my life. I have written more books, prepared more sermons, and have a large family comprised of four children in my home ranging from two to nine years old, whom I spend time with every day. I help with homework, do my work, handle everyday business, and travel the world, all in relation to getting up early to seek God. I come out of my study charged and ready to face the day. I implore you to set your alarm clock early in the morning and try it. If you do, you will begin to see the benefits almost immediately.

You may say, "Well, I'm not a morning person." Let me tell you who you are talking to. I have suffered from insomnia my entire life. I used to hate waking up in the mornings. I could never seem to get myself going, mainly because I could never get to sleep at night. Before I knew what was going on with me, I thought I was just a night owl. I wasn't a night owl, I was an insomniac. My insomnia has been cured since I started my 4:30 a.m. practice. I absolutely love waking up in the early hours of the morning. I promise you that you will find yourself popping out of the bed before the alarm goes off to spend time with God once you experience all the benefits that come from seeking Him early.

This was a common practice for Jesus as well. Mark 1:35 says, "*And in the morning, rising up a great while before day, He went out, and departed into a solitary place, and there prayed.*" Jesus was showing us the pattern for seeking God early and getting the infusion of strength and the download of information needed to start a new day. Let us endeavor to make this a part of our daily lives as well.

GOD'S DESIGN FOR YOUR LIFE

One of the greatest benefits of seeking God is that only through the One who created you can you understand why you were created. The primary place to start a vision quest is found within your time of prayer. You see, your vision begins with God and His ultimate design for your life. The place you cultivate a connection of communication with God is through your prayer time. When people tell me that they don't know their purpose and they don't know where to find it, I always ask them how much time they are spending in prayer. The reason is simple. When you seek the one who made you, He will reveal the reason you why He made you. Sometimes this comes through actually hearing His voice speaking to your spirit, or you may start to see events lining up and pointing in a certain direction in your life. This one thing I do know, and that is if you ask God to show you your purpose then He will. James 1:5–8 says,

> *If any of you lack wisdom, let him ask of God, that gives to all men liberally, and upbraids not; and it shall be given him. But let him ask in faith, nothing wavering. For he that wavers is like a wave of the sea driven with the wind and tossed. For let not that man think that he shall receive anything of the Lord. A double minded man is unstable in all his ways.*

When you seek the one who made you,
He will reveal the reason you why He made you.

Wisdom in this verse is the Greek word *sophia*, meaning "broad and full of intelligence, used of knowledge of very diverse matters." When you ask God in faith to reveal your purpose,

He gives you this knowledge as promised in the aforementioned verse. You have to ask yourself these questions: Why would God create me if not for a purpose? If He has created me for a purpose, then what would be His benefit in withholding this information from me? God wants to show you why you are here.

The age old question "What is the meaning of life?" is answered by doing what you have been created to do. You will only feel the sense of connection that you so desperately seek when you find out why you are here in the first place. The great thing about prayer is that it's the straightest and most direct way to come into contact with a living God and to discover who you really are. Isn't that what purpose is all about? It's about finding the real you. That's why you picked up this book. You were drawn to it because you felt like there was more to life than what you have been experiencing. You feel, on a deeper level, that you are out of balance with who you were created to be. You may be tired of being defined by your position at work or the limits of what you are currently doing, and for the first time you have found a way out of living an unfulfilled life. Only through establishing contact with God can this be done.

> **You will only feel the sense of connection that you so desperately seek when you find out why you are here in the first place.**

As we seek God, we discover that we really find ourselves. I want to suggest that many who are reading this book right now are in a state of wonder. Your life hasn't turned out the way you thought it would and you wonder why. I want to say to you that you have become exactly what you thought you would be. This has either happened consciously or unconsciously. What

I mean by this is that people become whatever they think they will become. When you have never been exposed to who you are in the first place then you simply become whatever is presented before you. If I didn't follow my calling, I would have probably worked in a fabricating shop like the rest of my family. And while there is certainly nothing wrong with that type of work, it's not what I was called to do. I was called to communicate hope to those that feel hopeless. If I didn't heed that call, I would have gravitated to whatever was before me. That's what happens when we don't take the time to get the specifics of God's plan for our life.

BOLD COMMITMENT TO THE VISION

I want you to know that God has incredible things ahead for you, but the first thing you need to do is find out what those plans are. When you do, you need to sell out to the vision that God places before you. Throw yourself into seeing the vision come to pass, because you will never feel a sense of wholeness until you fulfill God's design for your life. Does this scare you? Is your heart racing yet? Do you feel your palms getting sweaty? Good! That's the way life should be lived!

When you come out of the place of comfort it can be scary, but this is exactly what is required of a person of vision. You have to be willing to give your life to the vision or give nothing at all. It's time you actually decided to live for once. It's time that you took a chance and left the safety of where you currently are. You can be safe and feel lost at the same time. We were never created to play it safe; we were put here to be risk-takers and legend-makers. The true life of a visionary is the life of a champion. No matter what comes your way, you just keep on coming with a myopic view focused on the vision ahead.

I want to inspire you the way I was inspired when I was in the military. As I was going through training we were about to run an obstacle course. The instructor stood at the base of a massive tower that we had to climb and then descend from on a zip line. As he looked at our scared faces, he told us that it was his job to push us beyond what we thought we could do. Although I can still feel scared by a challenge, even after so many years, that statement still resonates with me today. I believe that God wants to push us beyond what we think we can do. This is exactly what the life of a person of vision entails. As they used to say on *Star Trek*, "To boldly go where no man has gone before."

> I believe that God wants to push us beyond what we think we can do. This is exactly what the life of a person of vision entails.

When we allow ourselves to dream, we see our heart's desire fulfilled. Psalm 37:4 says, *"Delight yourself also in the Lord: and He shall give you the desires of your heart."* Here once again is the key to this principle: our desire begins with God becoming our delight. It's important to understand what God means by *"desires"* here. I think that most of us have been left wanting because we have gotten exactly what we thought we wanted. The problem we face when we get what we want is that most times, our desires have been motivated by the wrong source. We get what we think we want instead of what God wants for us. Desires that are in alignment with God come from God, not from within ourselves.

When God created you He also put within you the desire to fulfill your mission here on earth. It's only when we seek Him for what He intends for us that we can truly be satisfied. It's amazing that your flesh, otherwise known as your ego, loves to have you chasing after things that are not good for you. The voice of your desires can sound so much like God's voice when you're not in tune with Him through prayer. How many times have you gotten into a relationship with someone based on how you felt? You just knew this person was "the one," only to have completely different feelings shortly thereafter. What happened? You were *so* convinced they were "the one." The problem is that the voice of your desire was drowning out the voice of God and His desire for your life. You see, God knew exactly what it would take for you to feel complete and whole when He created you. He placed His desires in you to realize those things and to experience them here on earth. It's only when you get back in contact with Him that you can come into alignment with what He desires for your life.

You may think that your desires for your life are "good enough" because you don't want to feel like you are settling for less in order to capitulate to God's desire for your life. This thought is born out of a spiritual disconnection. What a notion, that somehow, what you want could possibly be better than what God wants for you. The truth is that what God wants to do in your life far exceeds what you could ever desire. Ephesians 3:20 says, "*Now to Him that is able to do exceeding abundantly above all that we ask or think, according to the power that works in us.*" The moment a thought enters your mind about a desire, yet before you can articulate it with your mouth, God says that He is already doing more than your thought or spoken word. God's desire for your life is far beyond what you can even comprehend. This is why it is so important to connect with Him.

Notice that He says that this power is in you. This is another key to this principle. You have to realize that God isn't far away in another cosmos, where He's difficult to find. No, on the contrary, He's *within* you. So many times we practice the absence of God instead of the presence of God. This is because we don't realize that the power is already within us to connect with God and His superabundant purpose for our life.

> **God isn't far away in another cosmos,
> where He's difficult to find. No, on the contrary,
> He's *within* you.**

I want you to remember this as we prepare to close this chapter. You have a purpose for life and a reason for existing. God wants to reveal this purpose to you through the power of vision. That vision can only be revealed to you when you seek the One who designed your future before you ever got here. God has a plan for your life and that plan is available only when we find it in prayer.

PRAYER TIME WITH GOD

What He is telling me about my purpose.

_____

_____

_____

_____

_____

PRINCIPLE TWO

2

PRINCIPLE TWO:
OVERCOMING DOUBTS AND FEARS

One of the first things you will experience when you start this process of writing out your vision and visualizing a better future is doubt and fear. They will start to rise up within you. You will hear the voice of your past reminding you of all the times you have failed. You will hear fears tell you that these things you are envisioning may happen for others but not for you. You will feel emotions that run counter to what you have dreamed about and written down. Your excitement about a better future will be replaced with a sinking feeling that this will never happen in your life. I want you to know that this is normal.

The reason you will feel this way is because of the necessary process of challenging your old patterns of thought. These old patterns are normal for you and there is a sense of comfort in knowing where you currently are. You feel as if you understand the way life is, and there is a false sense of security in this knowledge. When you work the principles of vision, your old mindsets and familiar ways of thinking will have to change, and these set ways of thought and action won't go away easily.

> **When you work the principles of vision, your old mind-sets and familiar ways of thinking will have to change, and these set ways of thought and action won't go away easily.**

THE VOICE OF THE VISION VERSES THE VOICE OF FEAR

I find it amazing that we will fight to hold on to things that are unproductive in our lives, even when we aren't aware that this is what we're doing. That's why vision is so important! Your vision has a voice as well. I remember when I first started learning about this process. I was in the Army and my platoon sergeant told me that I should write out goals for what I wanted to happen over the next six months of my life. We'll look at this more in depth later, but this was my first experience with the power of vision. I wrote down several goals that I wanted to accomplish in that time frame. I posted them on the wall by my bunk and I soon discovered that as I looked at these goals every day, they began to speak louder than my doubts and fears. Pretty soon I no longer heard the doubts because I was seeing myself moving toward those goals and reaching milestones every day. Over that six-month period, I received a perfect score on my physical fitness test, I made the dean's list in college, I won several soldier and promotion boards, and I lost thirty pounds—all because the voice of my vision became louder than the voice of my fears.

I will show you in subsequent chapters how to take your goals and make them into statements that you speak every day, but for now I just want you to know that this does work. This principle will help you overcome the voices in your head telling you why you can't do something.

> **Many of the things we deal with are due to the fact that we don't ask for the things we want to happen in our lives. Instead, we complain, give up, or resign in our minds that things will never change and that there is nothing we can do about it.**

Paul gives us a powerful word of encouragement to be able to combat the voice of fear and doubt in Philippians 4:6–7, which says, *"Be anxious for nothing, but in everything by prayer and supplication, with thanksgiving, let your request be made known unto God; and the peace of God, which surpasses all understanding, will guard your hearts and minds through Christ Jesus"* (NKJV). I absolutely love this verse because of its all-encompassing nature. It covers every area of fear that one could possibly have and gives you the formula for overcoming that fear. Paul begins by acknowledging that anxiety is real and can be a problem for anyone who dares to dream for a better life. He's also telling us that life in general can and will produce anxious feelings. The great thing about this is that we don't have to succumb to these feelings, but instead, we are instructed to combat these feelings with prayer. In that prayer we are to make our requests known. Many of the things we deal with are due to the fact that we don't ask for the things we want to happen in our lives. Instead, we complain, give up, or resign in our minds that things will never change and that there is nothing we can do about it.

The good news is there *is* something you can do about fear. You can pray and make your request known to God, in faith, believing that He will bring your dreams to pass. The amazing thing about this verse is that what you pray about is an already-done thing. With the knowledge that God hears your prayer, you have an overwhelming sense of peace that what you have requested is happening as you pray. I often tell people not to stop praying about something until they feel peace about it. Once you have accepted the fact that what you requested is already yours, then you will feel the peace that goes beyond your comprehension. This is what I want you to see here. When you operate in the principles that govern vision, you may initially feel fear, but if you stay on course, you will have an internal knowing that it's only a matter of time before what you see in the sprit manifests in the natural. You can take this thought and knowledge and find your place of total peace. This state of bliss comes when you have prayed, made requests known, and found rest in the fact that it's only a matter of time until you see it showing up. There is a trust that comes in the all-powerful move of God to perform in your life, bringing His desire for you to completion.

Paul shares with us again about fear in 2 Timothy 1:7. The Bible says, "*God has not given us a spirit of fear, but of power and of love and of a sound mind*" (NKJV). The word for "*fear*" in the Greek is not the normal word for *phobia*. Instead this word is *deilia* and means "timidity, fearfulness, and cowardice." What the writer is trying to convey here is that God hasn't given us the spirit of a coward. When we step out on faith and dare to launch our vision, God will give us the courage to face whatever comes our way. Your vision will be tested; you will think about giving up; and all the reasons why it can't happen will be presented before you. This is all a part of the natural process of vision. The key is to remain steadfast in your resolve that what God promised you will ultimately happen no matter what. God will give you the courage to face your fears, overcome them, and then press into the desired results in your life.

> **Sometimes the best teacher for a courageous heart is failure. This is why it's so important that you put your past into proper perspective.**

BUILDING COURAGE, STAYING ENCOURAGED

Courage comes from the Latin word *cor*, which means "heart." This means that courage isn't something conjured up in a "fight or flight" scenario. Courage is something that is developed over time. Sometimes the best teacher for a courageous heart is failure. This is why it's so important that you put your past into proper perspective. If you look at the times when things didn't work out, you may lose heart. If, on the contrary, you see those events as necessary for your future development, and that the timing simply wasn't right, you will be encouraged that those moments served as your teachers so you would be ready to receive your destiny in the future.

The past affects our future because we think that things in the future will be like they have always been. Understand that your past was a part of the building blocks of your courage. It may not have worked then but it can certainly work now. Every time you failed in the past must become a stepping-stone of courage for the future, not a stumbling block. David knew that he had to stay encouraged even when the odds were stacked against him, because he knew that his past didn't dictate his future. First Samuel 30:6 says, "*And David was greatly distressed; for the people spoke of stoning him, because the soul of all the people was grieved, every man for his sons and for his daughters: but David encouraged himself in the LORD his God.*" David had just come home with his men and found that everyone was missing and the city had been burned to the ground. His own men wanted to kill him. Instead giving up or giving in, David took on a courageous spirit. Because he took this posture, they eventually recovered everything.

The next time you face a challenge in your vision, remember what David did. He kept his cool and encouraged himself. If everyone else is giving up, stay encouraged. If everyone turns their back on you, stay encouraged. Even if everyone is blaming you, stay encouraged. Encourage yourself so that God will see you through, and you will prevail with the victory regardless of the circumstances. Let's look again at the verse from 2 Timothy:

> God has not given us a spirit of fear, but of **power** and of **love** and of **a sound mind**." (2 Timothy 1:7 NKJV)

A SPIRIT OF POWER

In this verse, Paul notes the type of spirit God *does* give. He gives us power. This is important to remember whenever you face the fears that come with any movement toward your vision. You have to understand that God has empowered you to accomplish your goals. In the beginning, you may not see how something is going to work, or how it will ultimately turn out, but you have the power to see it through to the end. *Power* in the Greek is the word *dynamis*, meaning strength and ability. God will always give you the strength to stand up for your vision, even when your vision seems to be going in the opposite direction from what you originally envisioned. God will also give you the ability to execute everything needed to fulfill your destiny.

This is encouraging because I have found that God will always call you to dream beyond your current abilities and then empower you right when you need it to be able to do whatever it takes to see that vision happen. Richard Branson said, "If someone offers you an amazing opportunity and you're not sure you can do it, say yes—then learn how to do it later."[1] What an amazing way to view the point I'm trying to make here. You have to step out in faith for your vision, even when you aren't completely qualified yet. God will give you the ability as you go in order to accomplish what He has called you to do.

> **You have to step out in faith for your vision, even when you aren't completely qualified yet. God will give you the ability as you go in order to accomplish what He has called you to do.**

1. Richard Branson, "My top 10 quotes on opportunity," Virgin.com, https://www.virgin.com/richard-branson/my-top-10-quotes-opportunity, (accessed May 24, 2017).

I remember when I spoke for the first time in front of a large crowd. After that moment, I was asked to speak everywhere. The problem was that I wasn't very skilled at speaking in different places, night after night. I had to learn how preserve my voice, develop new material, and connect with different types of people in different settings. I knew when things started happening for me that I wasn't quite ready, nevertheless I went for it. I knew that what I needed would come, and it did. Years later, I'm still going strong because God empowered me and gave me the ability to fill the new shoes that were placed on my feet.

This is the key to vision, it forces you to grow and to expand. If you decide not to follow the principles in this book, you will remain in the same position you're in now. The moment you start to open up your view of possibility, you will be forced to grow and change. This is a good thing! Don't be afraid; know that God will give you the power to do this and succeed in the vision He has given you.

A SPIRIT OF LOVE

Love is the next thing mentioned in this verse. This might seem strange when talking about your vision until you understand the role love plays. Love is a part of the process of manifesting anything in your life. Think about it this way, according to 1 John 4:8, God *is* love. So we when we are attempting to reach into the spirit realm and bring that world into our natural form, we are grasping at a place that is pure love. The all-powerful originating Spirit of everything is God, and God is love. Therefore, to connect with His power, we must connect with Him on His level. That is why Galatians 5:6 says that faith works by love. The closer we can draw to the pure love of God, the stronger our connection to the Spirit will be.

Since we know that God created everything from the form-less place of Spirit, and that He brought it into being by love, we know that we can do the same in manifesting our vision when we operate in love. Hebrews 11:3 puts it this way: *"What is seen was not made out of what was visible"* (NIV). The only way to access this unseen realm is to do so through love. This is done when we take the time to fall in love with God by allowing His love to saturate us to such a place that we can love ourselves. The command in Mark 12:31 says that we should love our neighbor as we love ourselves. Therein lies the problem. We don't love our past, our present, or even the things in the future. We have low self-esteem, a low self-value, and we don't know how to be in tune with the greatness of God's creation, which includes us. So we have the wrong gauge by which to measure our love due to the fact that we don't love ourselves.

> **Love is a risk, and only when you see it this way can you really learn how to love the three most important entities of your affection: God, yourself, and your fellow human beings.**

Then, of course, the connection to God's love and the love we have for ourselves must extend to others as well. Eugene Lowry gives an example of the way love should be preached. He suggests that love isn't just something you tell people they should or shouldn't do. He writes, "The opening sermonic state-ment: 'Today I want to talk about love' is dull indeed until risk is introduced: 'Our problem is that so many times we extend our hand in love only to bring it back bruised and broken. To love is to risk rejection.'"[2] This is the proper way to preach love. Love is a risk, and only when you see it this way can you really learn how to love the three most important entities of your affection: God, yourself, and your fellow human beings. The reward for taking this risk is a life of manifested dreams. As we perfect love, we gain access into the divine and all that we purpose to do in the vision God has given us.

A SOUND MIND

Next we are told that God gives us a sound mind. This in the Greek is *sophronismos* and means discipline, self-control, and moderation. One of the most important aspects of divorcing the spirit of a coward is not only to operate in power and love, but also to have discipline. I believe that this is perhaps the most important and overlooked part of the vision process.

> **Daily discipline is the one thing that will outlast any attack on your vision and its future fulfillment.**

I have learned that whatever you go after will always be challenged. This is just a fact of life. If you want to see forward progress, you must understand that it takes force to get anything off the ground. Daily discipline is the one thing that will outlast any attack on your vision and its future fulfillment. There is a reason I run six days a week—it's the discipline in my commitment to the vision I have for my health. I know that if I run like this then I am able to manage my weight better, my emotions

2. Eugene Lowry, *The Homiletical Plot* (Louisville, KY: Westminster John Knox Press, 2001), 30.

stay in balance, and I even feel the benefit of this cardiovascular exercise when I speak. Believe it or not, when I'm active in my running discipline, I find myself wanting heathier food, which causes a nexus to form between what I do to exert the body and what I put back into it.

As I mentioned before, I have a daily discipline of prayer and study. This keeps me built up for any and all challenges I may face during the course of a day, and I, in turn, have loads of energy from this spiritual discipline. When you write a vision, you are also writing the things you are going to do to accomplish those goals. This is where your daily moderation has to become a lifestyle. One way to overcome doubt and fear is to create new habits that you perform on a daily basis. These new, positive habits will become the basis for the vision of your future.

> You can't expect to succeed in any area of your life without first having discipline in the areas that you are attempting to change. There must be a change in behavior as well as to your mind-set.

When I played football we had several habits. We did regular weight training, running, film study, and on-the-field practice. It takes a daily ritual to learn the mental side of the game and also to train your body for the physical side. You have to understand that having your head in the clouds with no discipline will lead to nothing. I want you to put you head in the clouds; I want you to dream big, but then I want you to develop habits that are congruous to what you want to see showing up in your life. You can't expect to succeed in any area of your life without first having discipline in the areas that you are attempting to change. There must be a change in behavior as well as to your mind-set.

OPERATING IN FAITH AND THANKSGIVING

Here is an important last thought on how to overcome doubts and fears. Mark 11:24 says, *"Therefore I say to you, what things soever you desire, when you pray, believe that you receive them, and you shall have them."* This verse stands as a powerful tool for you to shun doubt and fear and, instead, to operate in faith concerning your vision. If you can grasp what this verse is saying you can banish all doubt about your vision and receive your heart's desire. The question you must ask yourself is, "What will I have?" At first it looks like you will have your desire, but that's not it. There are a lot of people with desires that never see them come to pass. Next it looks like you have what you pray for, but, yet again, there are a lot of people praying and not getting what they pray for. Then it looks like you will have what you believe, but, once, again a lot of people believe for things and never receive them. So what is Jesus saying then? The end of the verse reveals what will cause the things we desire, pray for, and believe in to happen. It says that this will only happen if we believe that we receive them. Let that thought settle in your mind; *you will only get what you believe you have already received.*

One of the best ways to remove doubt and fear is to get to a place in prayer where you believe that you already have what you ask for. Think about it like this: the way a vision works is by faith; the way faith works is by believing that the object of your desire is already a reality before it ever shows up in your natural life. When you believe you have something in the Spirit, it should be your conclusion that you will see it show up in material form.

The key is to believe that this is true before it actually happens. One way to put this into practice is to think, act, and live as though what you have placed your faith in has already arrived. We began this chapter by looking at Philippians 4:6–7. In that verse, Paul affirmed that our prayer and supplication should be with thanksgiving. Thanksgiving is one of the ways in which we act as though we already have the things we are believing for.

> Paul affirmed that our prayer and supplication should be with thanksgiving. Thanksgiving is one of the ways in which we act as though we already have the things we are believing for.

If you asked me to give you my car and I agreed, I'd give you the title of ownership and the keys, and you would most likely respond by saying, "thank you" (if you are like most people). What you wouldn't do is keep asking me for my car. When you petition God for something, and you believe that you already have it, you don't need to keep asking for it because you believe He has already given it to you. Until it shows up, the next action to take is to thank Him for it as if it was a present reality. Not only can you thank God for it, but you can also praise Him as if you already have it. Some have said that you should praise Him in advance. This phrase "praise in advance" is a catchy term but is a little misleading because there is no advance on something that is already done. So what you are really doing is praising God as if it were yours right now. This is an incredible faith move on your part, one that puts you in alignment with what you believe you have already received. When doubt or fear tries to creep back in about what you have faith for, you can just revert right back to your place of praise and thanksgiving, and know that what you desire is already yours, and that is will show up at the perfect time.

PRAYER TIME WITH GOD

What are you thanking God for that you have already received?

_____

_____

_____

_____

_____

_____

_____

PRINCIPLE THREE

3

PRINCIPLE THREE:
VISUALIZE WHAT YOU DESIRE

I've always been told that as a preacher I needed "a vision." I wanted desperately to have one but no one ever showed me how to do actually do it. Therefore, I had to learn on my own what this vision business was all about. I want to share with you what I have learned and done in my life that has yielded tremendous results, because I know it can and will transform your life.

ENVISION YOUR FUTURE, WRITE DOWN WHAT YOU SEE

Visualizing what you desire and writing down what you see is the beginning phase of creating the type of life that you want to live. There's only one rule: you're not allowed to dream too small. You have to be willing to expand your mind and open up your heart to the fact that you serve a big God who wants to do something big in your life, even if other people don't think it's possible.

Last night I googled the phrase "do what you love and love what you do." The first search result was an article claiming this phrase was bad advice and should be ignored. I didn't read the article or even click on it because I knew that the one who wrote it, at some point in their life, must have given up on their dream and now they were telling everyone else that they have to live a mundane life, too. You will hear this a lot when you start on your own vision. You will be told all the reasons why you can't do it. You must learn to ignore the advice of well-meaning people who either failed or quit in pursuit of their own vision or never had the faith to try getting one at all.

> **The thing we must understand is that the things we call "failures" are actually our master teachers if we don't allow them to discourage us.**

I have a close relative who started a business and failed. In the beginning she was excited about the prospect of starting her venture, but after failing she was totally turned off by the idea and emphatically told me she would never do it again. Instead, she took a job unrelated to her original vision, where she has worked ever since. The thing we must understand is that the things we call "failures" are actually our master teachers if we don't allow them to discourage us. I expect failure, because I know it shows me the things I need to learn to ultimately succeed. If I would have quit every time I failed, I wouldn't be where I am today. I have failed more times than I have succeeded. Thankfully, I've used these failures to look for even greater opportunities, and they have always come.

> Contrary to popular belief, we can all thrive here on this planet. The only shortage of resources is the one we create in our minds and accept as our own reality. We can become whatever we were intended to become during our time on earth.

Like I said before, the only thing you can do wrong is dream too small. I want you to envision what you want your life to look like one year from now if everything you read in this book worked for you. Ask yourself what your ideal relationships would look like, what type of house you would live in, what kind of car you would drive, how much money you would make, and what you would do for a living. Think about the things you feel drawn to—your deepest desires that may seem beyond your reach right now. You may be saying to yourself that you're barely making it right now and that you just want to pay your bills on time. I certainly understand that, and that is built into the later stages of the vision process, but for now I want you to take the time to go beyond your current reality and see the future. See something bigger and more expansive. Dream with your eyes wide open and visualize what you want to become in the future.

I believe that we were all put here for a specific purpose and we all have a place in this world. Contrary to popular belief, we can all thrive here on this planet. The only shortage of resources is the one we create in our minds and accept as our own reality. We can become whatever we were intended to become during our time on earth. I truly believe that something (even if you're not sure of it yet) is calling to you. I believe that you don't find purpose, it finds you. All you need to provide for your purpose is available to you right now.

Right now, take time to ask yourself some in-depth questions about where you want to be in life. When I first asked myself these questions and wrote down answers, it was a liberating experience. I asked myself what I wanted to do for the rest of my life. I wrote out in great detail what my ministry looked like. I started by writing that I would preach in the International Holy Convocation. From there my ministry would be launched to a place where I would travel the world preaching and teaching in churches and conferences. I wrote that I wanted to be an author. I wanted to live the rest of my life sharing the Good News with the world. I wrote that I wanted to be a guest and a host on TV. Little did I know that over the course of the next two years, all of this would come to pass in my life. I would stand on the stage in front of the largest crowd I have ever encountered and preach on the very platform that I saw myself on when I was nineteen. After this, my ministry took off at such a rate that I had to leave my position on staff at a church to work full time as a speaker. I was subsequently on TV multiples times as a guest and later hosted several shows.

That's the power of vision! I also wrote down goals for my health as well. I dropped in weight from 230 pounds to 180 pounds in one year. That's a written vision in action, my friends. Nothing is off limits. You can write down where you want to be emotionally and spiritually. Any area of your life that you want to improve, you can. Right now, you probably feel something stirring within you. That's the hope that comes with the possibility that you can live at a higher level than what you are currently experiencing. This is what vision gives you—a solid hope for the future.

> **Right now, you probably feel something stirring within you. That's the hope that comes with the possibility that you can live at a higher level than what you are currently experiencing.**

Let's explore exactly how we should structure principle three of the vision process. Habakkuk 2:2 says, *"And the LORD answered me, and said, Write the vision, and make it plain upon tables, that he may run that read it."* I love the fact that this verse starts by saying, *"And the LORD answered me."* I want you to take the time to ask God exactly what He wants to do in your life. When you hear the answer, your response should be to write it down. Here are some things I want you to ask Him and yourself.

1. What do your relationships look like?

+ Your relationship with the Lord

_____

_____

_____

+ Your family

_____

_____

_____

+ Your spouse

_____

_____

_____

+ Your friends

_____

_____

_____

2. What do you do for a living?

+ What would you do if you could do anything and be paid for it?

_____

_____

_____

+ What is your ultimate calling?

_____

_____

_____

+ What type of work would make you feel as if you contribute to a better world?

_____

_____

_____

+ What does your typical day look like?

_____

_____

_____

3. What type of money do you make?

+ Get a figure in your head and double it because you are always worth more than you think.

_____

_____

_____

+ What does abundance look like to you?

_____

_____

_____

+ What do you have in your life?

_____

_____

_____

4. Where do you live?

+ Describe in detail what you house looks like.

_____

_____

_____

+ Write down what area it's in.

_____

_____

_____

+ Write down that you want to own it instead of rent or have a mortgage.

_____

_____

_____

5. What does your health look like?

+ What is your ideal weight?

_____

_____

_____

+ What type of exercise do you perform?

_____

_____

_____

+ What are your idea sugar, cholesterol, and other mea-
  surable levels at?

_____

_____

_____

+ How do you feel physically?

_____

_____

_____

6. How are you mentally and emotionally?

+ Describe in detail how you want to feel.

_____

_____

_____

+ List any problems you are dealing with such as anxiety or depression and write down the opposite of the struggles you are currently having.

_____

_____

_____

_____

_____

_____

This is a short outline that you can follow to get you started on the vision-writing process. These are just suggestions of what you can ask yourself, but there are no limits to what you can write. Any area of your life that you want to excel in can be written about in this stage of the vision process. Remember not to just look at your immediate needs but to focus on the big picture.

CHANGE YOUR PERSPECTIVE, EXPAND YOUR POSSIBILITIES

Before moving forward, let's take a closer look at Habakkuk 2. This chapter begins in the first verse by saying, *"I will stand upon my watch, and set me upon the tower, and watch to see what He will say to me, and what I shall answer when I am reproved."* The first thing we see here is that Habakkuk changes his location. He takes himself from a lower place to a higher elevation. I want us to look at this metaphorically, although I believe that he literally went to a higher place from a physical perspective. What I want you to understand is that he changed his vantage point. If we are going to get a vision for our future, then the first thing we must do is change our vantage point. When you can elevate yourself beyond the surface level of what you are experiencing right now in your current circumstances, and see beyond them from a place of elevation, then you can get a glimpse of the future possibilities that are ahead of you. You will never get a vision by looking at what is directly in front of you. You must elevate your view to a place of seeing beyond your current level and seeing into the future. This is the real definition of a visionary, someone who can see the future.

Next we see that the writer tells us that he will *"watch and see what he will say to me, and what I shall answer when I am reproved."* The word *"watch"* here is the Hebrew word *tsaphtah,* which means to look about, spy, keep watch, and observe. Habakkuk is telling us that he will spy out the future with what God reveals to him. As we learned earlier, we have the ability, through the daily practice of prayer, to have the plans of our future revealed to us. God will cause you to see what He has for you, and ultimately to become what you see. He also says that he will wait on the answer of God when he is reproved. Once again we see that through our connection to God in prayer that we are able to hear the answers to the questions of who we are and why we were placed on this earth.

He uses a strange word in latter part of this verse to describe the type of answer that he will receive. He says, *"when I am reproved."* *"Reproved"* is the Hebrew word *towechah*, which means to correct. This seems a little harsh if we take it as a punishment to the prophet. I think it is best understood as a *course correction*. When we elevate our minds and get a God-vision for our life, it corrects the path that we are currently on. It is widely known and documented that planes get off course most of the time during a fight. Because of this, there are constant slight adjustments during the flight to keep it on course. When we get our vision from God for our life, it's a correction that places us back on the path to our destiny, instead of hopelessly wandering on the wrong course. God wants us to elevate our view and He wants to give us the ability to see into the future. From this elevated place, He will show us what He has for us in the times to come. Then we must only wait for the instructions that bring His course correction to our lives. The written words that come from what you visualize are meant to cause you to change the direction you're going in and to put you in line with God's vision for your life.

> **When we get our vision from God for our life,**
> **it's a correction that places us back on the path to our destiny,**
> **instead of hopelessly wandering on the wrong course.**

Perhaps the concepts of principle three are best summed up by Psalm 133:1, which says, *"Behold, how good and how pleasant it is for brethren to dwell together in unity."* This is a verse I have heard quite a bit in my life. Usually it is used when there is a service at church in which all the local churches come together to worship. This is known as the unity verse for that very reason. I want to show you that this verse means so much more. It reveals to us the way in which we should approach our vision. It is believed by many scholars that David wrote this psalm before he became the king of Israel. This is significant, and I'll show you why in a moment. The word *"behold"* in the Hebrew is *chazah* and means to envision or see visions. Envision is defined as to think, conceive, imagine, realize, and to form an idea. David is telling us that he conceived a vision in his mind at this point. What did he see? Since he wasn't the king yet, he got a vision of his future kingship in his mind. He therefore looked out on an empty field and saw what he would become. He said, in essence, "Look at how good this will be when Israel comes together under my leadership." Herein lies the power of vision. It's the ability to see something that isn't visible in the natural and to capture that vision in your mind as if it's already a present reality. That's what David did and that's what you must do.

> **Herein lies the power of vision. It's the ability to see something that isn't visible in the natural and to capture that vision in your mind as if it's already a present reality.**

I want you to go to that elevated place of seeing into your future. Ask God to reveal what you will become in all areas of your life. Ask yourself what your life will look like by this time next year. Dormant facilities in your brain will be activated in you as you do this exercise. You will start to see things lining up in your life that seem like coincidences, but it's actually God working things in divine order to fulfill your dreams.

Second Corinthians puts it this way, "*While we look not at the things which are seen, but at the things which are not seen*" (2 Corinthians 4:18). You have to understand that your vision, by faith, produces things. Hebrews 11:1 tells us as much when it says, "*Now faith is the substance of things hoped for, the evidence of things not seen.*" Your vision is an expression of your faith, and your faith creates the things of your future. The problem we face is looking beyond what we see now. You have to understand that the rest of 2 Corinthians 4:1 says, "*The things which are seen are temporal; but the things which are not seen are eternal.*" When we visualize our future and write down what we see, we must understand that what we are currently experiencing is a result of what we have focused on in the past. That's exactly where these things need to be categorized and left…in the past. What you see right now is transient and was not intended to be permanent. When you get a vision and begin to dream about your future and what you can become, you tap into eternity. When you bring this portion of eternity from the unseen realm, then things you produce are with you forever because they are eternal. You can't repossess them; you can't foreclose on them; you can't lose them. Why? Because it comes from a real place that's nonlinear and outside of time.

God is urging us to look into the future and capture a vision of what we can become. Then He wants us to write it out and make it plain. You can do this by asking yourself some of the questions above, or by simply asking yourself what it is that you want. Don't look at your current temporary situation as a gauge. If you do, you will remain stuck in a cycle of repeating the same things over and over. Instead, see into the future and fix your spiritual eyes on a higher plane. Find that heavenly divine spark that will ignite your passion for the future and motivate your life to meet that end.

Before I started writing a series of books, I got a vision of what writing looked like for me. I didn't want to be a self-published author because I really wanted to have my material published and distributed to retail stores. So I looked into my future and thought about what that would that look like. After visualizing this and writing it down on paper, something very interesting happen to me. I was at a conference in Orlando and was scheduled to have lunch with the leader of the host group. When I was placed in the car, two other people were already in it, two friends of mine: Bishop Dale Bronner and his wife. During the ride, I had a conversation about some things that God had been dealing with me about. As I told them about this on the ride over they said that I should write a book about what I was sharing. Little did I know, my friend's publisher was with him on the trip and I was introduced to him. It took some time for me to write the first book, but when I submitted it I was given a three-book deal. Currently, I have submitted two of the three larger books and I'm writing this book as a fourth book, to serve as a prelude to the release of the others. All of this came about because I was willing to do what I'm asking you to do.

You have to see yourself in the future and believe that you can become what you see. It doesn't matter what your dream is. If you can see it, then you can be it. If you take what you see in your mind and put it on paper, miraculous things start to happen. One reason this is so important is because when you visualize and then write down what you see, you make a powerful impression on your subconscious mind. This part of your mind is the place where plans are produced. If you just go through life without a written vision, then your mind will keep giving you plans based on what you have always believed. When these beliefs are not challenged, they become the very reason why you are where you are. You are broke because you have never challenged this notion of lack in your life. You may be sick because you have always thought that this is how things have to be. Your subconscious mind creates plans to bring you the same results in your life. When you start to renew your mind with God's Word, and with the vision God has for your life, then your subconscious mind starts to produce plans for the accomplishment of your vision. You are about to see things so clearly, including the path that leads you to the fulfillment of your dreams, that you are going to wonder where this has been your entire life.

> **If you can see it, then you can be it.**
> **If you take what you see in your mind and put it on paper,**
> **miraculous things start to happen.**

So take the time now to write out in detail exactly what you want your life to look like in the future—and then watch God bring it to pass.

_____

_____

_____

_____

_____

PRINCIPLE FOUR

4

PRINCIPLE FOUR:
WRITING YOUR GOALS

Goal setting is the next step in the vision-writing process. Goals become the targets that you will pick out within your overall vision. If you wish to see the grand vision become a reality, you must first be able to break them down into workable parts. A quote attributed to Mark Twain reads, "The secret of getting ahead is getting started. The secret of getting started is breaking your complex overwhelming tasks into small manageable tasks, and then starting on the first one." This beautiful wisdom is the key to getting started on the fulfillment of your vision. What you will be doing in this chapter is taking the grand picture that you see and making it a little more manageable with goals.

GOALS ACTUALIZE VISIONS

Before I show you how to find the goals to work toward in your vision, let's take a look why we need goals. Proverbs 13:16 says, "*A wise man thinks ahead; a fool doesn't and even brags about it!*" (TLB). We are told in this verse of the importance of thinking ahead, of planning, and goal writing. Setting goals for yourself is one of the smartest things you can do because it keeps you from wondering aimlessly through life. When you think ahead, you will eventually get ahead. I love this quote by Mary Anne Evans, under her pen name George Eliot, which says, "It's never too late to be what you might have been." Goals give you the mark for which you should aim your life. They are the first part of a line that we will eventually lead from your goals toward the actualization of what you desire to manifest in your life, and toward becoming the person you were always meant to be.

> **When a person has their life centered on goals, and when they become committed to the fact that what they intend *will* happen, then it will always lead to prosperity.**

Proverbs 21:5 says, "*The plans of the diligent lead to profit as surely as haste leads to poverty*" (NIV). When a person has their life centered on goals, and when they become committed to the fact that what they intend *will* happen, then it will always lead to prosperity. Show me where you are lacking in your life and I'll show you a place void of the visionary aspect of goals. If you want to be locked into a life of never-changing cycles, then live by default and you will spend the rest of your days reacting to whatever comes your way. If, however, you start living a life driven by goals, then you will see profound changes start to happen in your life.

I told you earlier that when I was in the military I had my first encounter with goal writing. I will never forget the sheer power of those goals that I pinned on the wall of my barracks. They talked to me every day from the page torn from a notebook and written in black ink. It was amazing because sometimes they made me mad. When I wanted to be lazy or take the day off, there they were talking to me. It was as if they became my coach and my motivating force, pushing me to achieve what I had written down. They also came as words of encouragement and gave me a sense of movement in my life. Forward movement is a vital part of the vision process because it means that you are headed in a forward direction. Albert Einstein said, "Nothing happens until something moves." That's what goals do—they get you moving. That's certainly what my goals serve to do, even at this stage in my life. Never underestimate the power that a goal carries—it can propel you into action that leads to results.

A CHANGE IN PERCEPTION

The great thing about goals is that they help to change your perception. Perception is the number one determining factor of what we will see for our lives. This can be seen in the way natural vision works. I have studied vision extensively and I am amazed at the way in which natural and spiritual vision parallel one another. Hermann von Helmhotz discovered that what we see is based primarily on what we perceive. These preconceived notions, he discovered, affect the way we view what comes through the lens of our pupil and into our brains. If you change the perception, you can change what you see. This can be seen in the minds of those who have been raised in an environment where they are taught hate based on someone else's religious beliefs or the color of their skin. Only when these misperceptions are exposed to other cultures on a visceral level can change begin to occur. The key to changing what we see is through the new information we are exposed to. Only when how we think about something changes can we really see what it truly is.

William Blake said, "If the doors of perception were cleansed everything would appear to man as it is, Infinite. For man has closed himself up, till he sees all things thro' narrow chinks of his cavern." When we can change our perceptions, we can shape our minds in new ways. We can transform ourselves from our limited view and see the world through a new looking glass. Writing out goals will challenge the preconceived notions of what we thought about our life and open us up to infinite possibilities. I know that it is impossible to change your life without first changing your thoughts. What you think will eventually flood your actions and become the change agent that has eluded you up to this point. Your goals change your perception about what is possible, and, oftentimes, that's all you need to change your life in the direction of hope, health, abundance, and peace.

> **When we can change our perceptions, we can shape our minds in new ways. We can transform ourselves from our limited view and see the world through a new looking glass.**

Goals have the power to not only change your perception, but also to correct the ways in which you view your life and your potential. With natural vision, you have two eyes and two retinas, which cause you to have double vision—two eyes create two images. There is a part of the brain that lies between the right and left hemispheres called the corpus callosum. One of the functions of this part of the brain is to take the two images that you see and merge them into one.

I want to suggest that we all have double vision when we get to the place of the vision process where we write down our goals. The reason for this is because, as I said in chapter three, we all have doubts and fears. Some of them have been so engrained in our minds that we find it difficult to overcome them and see the possibility of a different life experience. So what we have is double vision. We have a set of goals telling us that everything is possible to us when we dare to dream, and then we have the images of our past, present, and future failure. When we start writing out goals, we are forced to contrast our fears with our dreams. Only when we have a functioning spiritual corpus callosum can we merge these two images together. This is the place where we start to see everything that has happened to us up to this point as a part of God's divine plan. We are no longer led by our past pain, mistakes, or failures. We have an internal *knowing* that everything happens for a reason and that everything we have been through in our past is working to promote a better future. From this vantage point, what we have seen as destructive in the past merges with our current goals and becomes a part of the driving force that creates change in our life.

Once again, we can draw a parallel between natural and spiritual vision when we examine the way in which an image is projected onto the movie screen of the mind. When an image comes in through the eyes and is projected onto the retina, the image is inverted. That's right, we all have double vision and we all see upside down. There is a portion of the brain that takes the upside down image and turns it right-side up. This is exactly what happens when you decide to write out goals for your life.

I have discovered that whenever I put my pen to paper, everything I write is in direct opposition to the way my life looks currently. I never seem to have enough money to complete the goal at that time of my life. This is because a God-goal extends beyond your ability to make it happen. No matter how much money you currently have, God will give you a goal beyond wherever you are financially. At this stage your money is upside-down. You may not have enough friends or connections to make your goals a reality, so your friends are upside-down. You may not have enough talent or education, so that is upside-down as well. The good thing is that within each of us is the Spirit of the living God. This Spirit has the ability to take what is upside-down and turn it right-side up. If you stay the course that your visionary goals have charted for you, you will see all the inverted images put back in their proper alignment in your life.

> **A God-goal extends beyond your ability to make it happen. No matter how much money you currently have, God will give you a goal beyond wherever you are financially.**

This is what you have to do when you write your goals and everything seems upside-down. Take the advice of Virginia Woolf: "Arrange whatever pieces come your way." This simply means that as the opportunities come they may be upside-down, or they may be incomplete as pieces to a larger puzzle. The key is to take what comes your way, put it in proper order, and trust God's divine direction to eventually send everything you need to reach and fulfill you written goals. God will take everything that is upside-down and, in time, turn it all right-side up.

> **If you stay the course that your visionary goals**
> **have charted for you, you will see all the inverted images**
> **put back in their proper alignment in your life.**

FINDING GOALS IN YOUR VISION

Let's take a look at how to find and write out our goals using our broad written vision. Remember that this vision is the expansive dream in written form that will become the basis for the smaller parts of the vision, which are our goals. What you are looking for in your vision are ways to sum up what you want in a short phrase that your mind can work with. Take for example some of the things that I had in my first vision, and how I wrote my original goals.

One of the sections I wrote about of course was what I wanted my ministry to look like. My vision looked something like this:

I am preaching in the International Holy Convocation for the Church of God in Christ. I have speaking engagements that take me all over the world, and I do this full time. I am able to support my family doing what I love.

This is just a small excerpt of what I would have written regarding what I wanted to do for the rest of my life. I went into great detail about what it would look like in my vision. I knew that I couldn't possibly think that my mind could wrap itself around all these details every day. It was important that I wrote out the details in order to determine the specifics of what I wanted to happen, but I needed something to work with. So I summed up this overarching theme of ministry that was in great detail with this simple goal:

GOAL:
SUCCESS IN PREACHING AND DOING WHAT I LOVE.

I hope you can see that this simple phrase encapsulates all that I was saying in the details I wrote in my vision. That's the key to goal writing: the ability to take the wordiness of what you have written in your vision and make it plain and workable for your daily use. We will see in the subsequent chapter that this is important in the confession part of our process, as well, because we will take these short phrases that carry the weight of the written vision and turn them into confessions we say on a daily basis. For now, though, I just want you to focus on simplifying your vision with your goals.

_____

_____

_____

GOAL:
MILLION-DOLLAR HOME OVER THE MOUNTAIN.

Another part of my written vision was about the house I wanted to live in. I wrote in great detail about wanting to live "over the mountain" in a million dollar home. I wrote that I wanted a circular driveway, a swimming pool, a Jacuzzi, a multi-car garage, a full living space for my mother, a Viking stove, and many other features. I wrote out exactly what I wanted in my dream home. Once again, this simple phrase captures all that I was saying in the vision and puts it into easy-to-understand, workable terms. When you do this part of the process, you send a powerful message to your mind that you have set yourself on a course to have the life you desire, and it sets specific targets in order to do just that.

Once again, I want to you to ignore those voices in your head telling you this will never work for you. Hearing those things is expected and a part of the process. You have to tell your fears that you have nothing to lose. Your life was going nowhere before, so if you go through this process and nothing changes, you haven't lost a thing; you'll just be back where you were when you started. Then tell yourself that this *could* happen, and that people live out their dreams every day. If God did it for them, He can certainly do it for you. You can live a life that sees your vision come to pass in miraculous ways. Things can and will begin to line up for you in perfect ways as you follow the path God has for you that leads you to the fulfillment of your vision. Dare to take the vision you have written, and identify the goals that will give you something to shoot for in your future.

_____

_____

_____

GOAL:
DRAWING CLOSER TO JESUS EVERY DAY IN PRAYER AND STUDY.

I took what I had written in my vision and once again broke it down into a simple phrase that my mind could use with intention for my future.

In my first vision (and every other vision since then) I wrote about my relationship with the Lord. I wanted to draw closer to God and have a more connected life to Him. I wrote that I wanted to spend at least one hour a day in prayer and one or more hours a day in study. As I said before, this has extended far beyond an hour and compels me to wake up at 4:30 a.m. every morning, before anyone else in my house wakes up. I get up this early because I need more than one hour now, because that place in me has expanded beyond my initial allotted time.

You see, I wanted to connect with God on a deeper level and I knew that this would require spending time talking to Him and learning more about Him. My goal seemed to bring together all that I had written into a quick and concise phrase that I could use to remind myself of all that I had written in my vision.

_____

_____

_____

GOAL:
HEALTHY 180 POUNDS.

This is the simply stated goal that matched what I had written in detail about my health. Before writing out my vision, I was in my early thirties, I already had high cholesterol, and I was overweight. I topped out at 235 pounds at one point and was severely unhealthy. So in my vision I included what I wanted to look and feel like from a health perspective. I wanted to eat healthy food and ingest things that were in line with the health I wanted to create in my life. I wrote that I wanted to run five miles a day to maintain good cardiovascular strength. I wrote that I would reach my ideal weight for my height and body style, which was 180 pounds.

In this short description of my detailed vision, I was once again able to give myself something that I could wrap my mind around. I knew when I wrote down this goal that I would eventually obtain it. Just like the goals of my military days, these goals and the others I wrote down spoke to me every day. Sometimes the goal motivated me, other times it inspired me. The one constant thing that my goals always did was push me to take action. We will discover as this book unfolds that this is the key to seeing your goals become a reality.

_____

_____

_____

GOAL:
I'M A LOVING, KIND, AND EMOTIONALLY BALANCED PERSON.

One of the other things I wrote in my vision was the type of person I wanted to be. In my life, like many of you, I have suffered great pain. I never knew my real father and that created a void in my life that I unknowingly struggled with for most of life. This persistent but covert problem lay at the base of everything that I struggled with on an emotional level. I had trouble trusting people because of the rejection I felt from being unwanted, and because of having a stepfather that didn't show me love either. When I wrote the portion of my vision that dealt with me and the type of person I wanted to be, I realized that I would need healing in this area. Through confronting these issues and working through them, I saw myself becoming what I had written down in my vision. I spelled out in detail that I wanted to be a kind, loving, compassionate, and emotionally secure person. I wanted to live my life from a perspective of love, joy, and peace.

This simplified goal statement has served me well by reminding me to always respond to people in loving and kind ways and to have compassion on those who are dealing with difficulties in their lives and are in need of help. One of the greatest joys that you will ever experience is when you have goals that are centered not only on health and abundance, but on your character and how you may contribute to a better world. In the end, that's the real need that we have for visionaries—to become people who touch the world with who we are and what we do. Your vision should be so large that it goes beyond you and blesses your generation and those to come. Take the information you have written out about what kind of person you want to become and write out a simple goal that captures the essence of that.

One place to start is by finding the things that you have labeled as a part of who you are. You know, the things that you make excuses for, by saying, "That's just the way I am." The truth is, you don't have to be any kind of way. Sure, you are born with a certain type of personality to fulfill a certain purpose, but I'm talking about those parts of yourself that keep you from connecting with other people. When you challenge the things that you consider to be *normal* for you, then you can start to develop better ways of living your life in connection to God and others.

_____

_____

_____

In this chapter, we have learned the importance of taking our massive and detailed vision and turning it into simple goals that we can use as markers and guides to lead us to the fulfillment of that vision. Remember that the mind does better when presented with headlines instead of all the details. You can trust that your mind knows that the details have already been written and will be taken care of. Your mind knows that you have all the information to support what you've written in your vision. Therefore, you can have confidence that your goals carry the full weight of what you have written. Take the time now to pull out the goals that will be the aim for your life from this moment forward, and then watch them talk to you as they motivate you toward their fulfillment.

PRINCIPLE FIVE

5

PRINCIPLE FIVE:
SPEAK IT

Once we have written our expansive vision and extracted specific goal statements, which are a condensed version of our vision, we have to take the next step. The next phase of the vision process builds on the last step. Next I will teach you the principle of taking your goals and turning them into positive confessions that you can say on a daily basis. When you master this principle, you will become intimate with your goals, because they will become an everyday part of your self-talk. Before I show you how to actually transform your goals into confessions, let's take a look at why what we speak is so important.

THE POWER OF THE TONGUE

Proverbs 18:21 says, *"Death and life are in the power of the tongue: and they that love it shall eat the fruit thereof."* The first thing I want to draw your attention to is that this verse begins with death. This, to me, is significant and is no accident. It is man's natural inclination to speak death first. We have been so conditioned to think the worst and expect the same that we are programed to respond this way initially. This is a fallacy that must be addressed and reversed if we are going to see our vision come to pass in our lives. We have to retrain our minds to see things from a positive frame of mind and not from the position of the negative. We have to shut out the external voices of friends and family that only want to tell us why something can't work rather than why it can. We have to find out what beliefs we are still holding on to that cause us to think death before life. Then we can move forward to the other option, which is speaking life.

> It's time that you change the way you speak forever.
> Before you give power to a negative thought,
> pause and think about it. Make a conscious decision that you
> will chose to speak life instead of death.

This proverb tells us that we have this power in our tongues. Power, according to this verse, is the Hebrew word *yad* and means hand. So the writer is telling us that what we choose to speak out of our mouths is what we will eventually have in our hand. It is amazing to think that it all comes down to this. We have the ability to speak death or life over our experience. It's time that you change the way you speak forever. Before you give power to a negative thought, pause and think about it. Make a conscious decision that you will chose to speak life instead of death. You can choose to speak sickness or you can choose to speak health. You can speak lack or abundance. You can speak bad relationships or healthy ones. Mind you, I'm aware that when you begin to do this you have to resist speaking of what you are currently experiencing. This can be difficult in the beginning, but soon you will see your life turning in the direction of what you say instead of what you see right now.

The next verse I want to look at is Job 22:28, which says, *"You shall also decree a thing, and it shall be established to you: and the light shall shine upon your ways."* We should learn from this verse once again of the power we have in our words. The writer here tells us that we can decree a thing. *"Decree"* is the Hebrew word *gazar*, meaning to cut, divide, cut off, or separate. So what we can draw from the original text is that our words have the power to cut through any obstacle in our lives and create exactly what we speak. The Hebrew word for *"established"* is *quwm*, which means to rise, stand up, and become powerful. So when we decree and cut down the blocks in our life, from that place of cutting, what you say will rise up. It will become powerful in your life. Just as our previous verse says, *"death and life are in the **power** of your tongue."* We have to understand that when we speak over our life and into our future, we are taking our place of authority and power as a believer. This place of power according to the rest of Job 22:28 creates a light that shines on our path. When you have a vision from God and you speak that vision, a spotlight shines on the next steps to the completion of that vision. As you decree what you will be, you will have a guiding light to lead you on the path to your destiny.

> **When you have a vision from God and you speak that vision, a spotlight shines on the next steps to the completion of that vision. As you decree what you will be, you will have a guiding light to lead you on the path to your destiny.**

It's so important that we allow our vision to sink deep within our hearts and minds. This is key because what is *in us* is what will come *out of us*. Jesus said, in Luke 6:45, "*A good man out of the good treasure of his heart brings forth that which is good; and an evil man out of the evil treasure of his heart brings forth that which that which is evil: for of the abundance of the heart his mouth speaks.*" We see then from this verse that our mouths are connected to our hearts. What we say is a direct reflection of what we are. If we speak doubt and unbelief, it's because that's what's in our hearts. Vision serves us to get our hearts in alignment on a personal, financial, physical, and spiritual level. When we conform to what we write in our vision, our hearts begin to conform to what is written. When this happens, we will speak what we have dreamed of instead of what we have feared. Get your heart right and the rest will follow, including your tongue. That's why Proverbs 23:7 says, "*For as he thinks in his heart, so is he.*"

THE POWER OF CONFESSIONS

The next thing I want to share with you is what confessions are and why we need them. The goals that you wrote out for the last principle are the beginning stages of this principle because they will be used as the basis for what you will say each day. The idea of confession is rooted in the Bible. Before we explore this idea let's take a look at this in relation to creation.

The first thing we must grasp is that we were all created in the image of God. The question then becomes this: What is that image? God was a Spirit who spoke the world into existence. Therefore, if we were created in His image, then we should also do what He did and speak our world into existence. The writer of Hebrews put it like this: *"Let us hold fast the confession of the hope unwavering, (for he [is] faithful who has promised;)"* (Hebrews 10:23 DARBY). Here, we are told that our faith can become our confession. When we attempt to step out on our vision by faith, we do so armed with the power of our confessions and know that what we are believing for in our vision will happen, just as we have spoken. Once again the apostle Paul says, *"We having the same spirit of faith, according as it is written, I believed, and therefore have I spoken; we also believe, and therefore speak"* (2 Corinthians 4:13). It is in the spirit of faith that you become a person that speaks what you believe. It's important to know that this is the very essence of what faith is. That is, believing and then speaking. So as we convert our goals into confessions, we need to know that we are exercising our faith at the highest level, and that this will create a new connection between what you desire and what you receive.

PRESENT-TENSE CONFESSIONS

Now that we understand how impactful our words are and why we should speak positive confessions, let's examine how we should speak our vision. Everything that God does is always "in the now." While you are sitting here reading this book, you are in the moment of now. *Now* isn't governed by the past or the future and it's the place where God resides. If we are going to receive anything from a God who is an eternal *now*, we must be able to respond to Him where He is, which is always in the present moment. Therefore, when we speak our goals as confessions they must be spoken in the present tense.

> **If we are going to receive anything from a God who is an eternal *now*, we must be able to respond to Him where He is, which is always in the present moment.**

Since our goals are confessions of our faith, we must follow the pattern of what faith is. Hebrews 11:1 says, "**Now faith is....**" Right from the beginning of what faith is we discover the time period that governs it. It is in the same realm as God, who sees everything as complete and is accessed on this level of being already done. So when we speak anything by faith we must speak it as if we already have what we are speaking. The psalmist put it this way in, "*Save now, I beseech You, O LORD: O LORD, I beseech You, send now prosperity*" (Psalm 118:25). The writer here is perfectly framing when we should place our confession of faith. He states, "*Save now....*" Did he immediately get deliverance from his situation? Probably not, but that didn't sway him, because you must speak what you desire as if you already have it, regardless of where you currently are in life.

He goes on further to ask God to "*send now prosperity.*" Notice that he didn't first talk about how broke he was or how much debt he was in; no, he spoke exactly what he desired, as if he already had it. It's interesting to note that the word "*beseech*" is the Hebrew word *anna*, and means "ah, now!" or "oh, now!"

It's as if the writer is saying to God, "Come on, Lord, it's about time this happened in my life." It also means, "pray now." So we are told to do this all in the Spirit of our Father, who is in the now. In order to put this powerful principle of speaking into practice, it must always be done from the place of the present.

Let's take a look at the goals I listed in the last chapter and I'll give examples of how to change them into confessions that are spoken in the now. One more thing on the structure of the confession before we move forward—not only should they be spoken in the now, but they also should be spoken as if they are in the process of happing. I use the word *succeeding* in my confessions because I want to speak them as if they're already done, and as if I am successful at receiving the completion of what I believe I have.

The first goal I created from our vision was concerning what I wanted to do for a living. My goal was: *Success at preaching and doing what I love.* What I want to do with this goal, as I previously stated, is to turn it into something that I speak into existence as if I already have it. So my confession would look like this:

CONFESSION:
I AM NOW SUCCEEDING AT PREACHING AND DOING WHAT I LOVE TO DO.

As you can see, this confession is written as simply as the goal, but with a few things added in order that it may be spoken daily as if it's already acquired. Notice that I added the phrase "I am…." This is important because we are speaking here about what we believe we already are. The best way to understand this is to understand who God is and where He resides. God is in everything and is everywhere, at all times—including in you. So if the great "I AM" that was revealed to Moses is in you, then you are what He is, and you are what He desires for your life. I was already a successful preacher before I ever had success at doing what I loved. It was already in me because God is in me, and He is everything at all times. When I wrote out my confession, I acknowledged what I already was because He already is and He was in me the entire time. My confession allowed me to access who I am, which is a part of who He is. In this way, I am whatever He destines for me to be at all times in my life, even before I know it. It is, and was always, within me my entire life. An acorn contains everything in it to become an oak, even though its current form doesn't yet reveal it. Confessions help what's inside of you to manifest on the outside.

_____

_____

_____

CONFESSION:
I AM NOW SUCCEEDING AT HAVING A MILLION-DOLLAR HOME "OVER THE MOUNTAIN."

Notice once again that I am simply taking my goal and turning it into something that I speak in the now.

_____

_____

_____

CONFESSION:
I AM NOW SUCCEEDING AT DRAWING CLOSER TO JESUS EVERY DAY.

CONFESSION:
I AM NOW SUCCEEDING AT WEIGHING A HEALTHY 180 POUNDS.

CONFESSION:
I AM NOW SUCCEEDING AT BEING A LOVING, KIND, AND
EMOTIONALLY BALANCED PERSON.

Those are examples of how to take a goal and turn it into a confession. I want you to go through every goal you have written out and do this exercise with them. What this does is take the targets, which are your goals, and turn them into powerful tools for reshaping your future. This is so vital because we become what we come from by engaging in this divine act of writing and speaking our confessions.

GOAL 1

_____

_____

_____

GOAL 2

_____

_____

_____

SPEAK YOUR FUTURE INTO EXISTENCE

We are told in Romans 4:17 that God *"calls those things which be not as though they were."* What a life-altering statement about our God. He starts His creative speaking by taking something that is not and speaking it as if it were. We see this in Genesis 1:2–3: *"Now the earth was formless and empty, darkness was over the surface of the deep, and the Spirit of God was hovering over the waters. And God said, 'Let there be light,' and there was light"* (NIV). This is a prime example of the exact way God responds to things that are not yet what they will become.

Hebrews 11:3 solidifies this thought even further by stating, *"By faith we understand that the universe was formed at God's command, so that what is seen was not made out of what was visible"* (NIV). What we see here in these two verses is that God doesn't consult what is seen when speaking anything into form. Instead,

He accesses the unseen part of the universe, from which we all materialized into form.

In this same way we all have been created in His image, we all have the power to access the world of Spirit and speak it into existence in our earthly lives. When we do this, we are following in the footsteps of our Lord and doing what He did. This is the ultimate expression of our faith. In fact, a person can't even receive Christ without first confessing Him as Lord. Romans 10:9 says, *"If you shall confess with your mouth the Lord Jesus, and shall believe in your heart that God has raised Him from the dead, you shall be saved."* Confession is our access into the kingdom, and it is our continued access into seeing our goals happen in divine ways in our earthy lives.

> **Confession is our access into the kingdom, and it is our continued access into seeing our goals happen in divine ways in our earthy lives.**

We need only to look out on the empty void of the earth as God did and see with our spiritual vision what we want to manifest and then speak it into existence. Don't complain about how things look now, *speak to it!* Don't talk about how bad it seems now, *speak to it!* Speak to it as if you already have it, and soon you will. What a wondrous thought that before God created the sun or the moon He was able to manifest light. How did He do this? First John 1:5 says, *"God is light, and in Him there is no darkness at all."* When God spoke, He just spoke what He already is—light. This is exactly what I want you to do. I want you to understand that God is already health, abundance, joy, peace, and anything thing else that is in tune with His nature. So when we speak things into existence, we are simply speaking what we already are in God.

Colossians 3:3 says, *"For you died, and your life is now hidden with Christ in God"* (NIV). When we die to ourselves and our way, and when we surrender, then we can connect with the vision God has for us that is found hidden in Him. This word *"hidden"* in the Greek is *krypto*, and means to conceal, escape notice, or to keep secret. This means that all of the failures of your past are no longer a factor, because they are hidden in God. Yet, through Him, we can live a life that is expressing itself in wonderful ways through the One with whom we are hidden. What He is, simultaneously, is what you are. If He is health then you are health; if He is abundance then you are abundance. That's the reason we speak our confessions as if we are what they say we are, because that is the only logical conclusion. That is, we are in God and God is in us. All matter in the world came from God and the unseen realm of the Spirit. Once we connect to the One who created us and all living things, then we connect to what we are as well. God created us and lives in us; therefore we are what He is. Paul said, *"But whoever is united with the Lord is one with him in spirit"* (1 Corinthians 6:17 NIV). Since we are united and one with Him, we can access and manifest whatever He is in our lives.

SCRIPTURE AS A CONFESSION TOOL

If you are tired of seeing and then speaking based on what you currently see or have always seen in your life, then it's time for you to shift your speech. You need to take this principle and apply it to every area of your life. Begin to speak what you want to happen and not what is happening. In Joshua 1:8, it says,

"This book of the law shall not depart out of your mouth but you shall meditate therein day and night, that you may observe to do according to all that is written therein: for then you shall make your way prosperous, and then you shall have good success."

Not only should you make confessions around the goals you have set, goals that were formed from the God-inspired vision for your life, but you should also use the Word of God as a tool of confession. The writer here is urging us first to make sure that the Word of God never leaves our mouth. We are told that the key to success and prosperity is found in speaking the Word. We are instructed to meditate on it day and night until it becomes what we say. When you can fashion your thought life around the Word it also becomes imbedded in your mind. What you place in your mind is what you will say, and what you say is ultimately what you will become.

> **When you can fashion your thought life around the Word it also becomes imbedded in your mind.**
> **What you place in your mind is what you will say, and what you say is ultimately what you will become.**

I have listed here, for your convenience, some verses that cover different areas of your life in confession form. You can find even more by searching with an online concordance or topical Bible.

Abundance:

- According to Proverbs 10:22, I am now succeeding at being rich with no sorrow.

+ According to Proverbs 11:25, I am now a liberal soul and I am increased; I help others and I am helped.

+ According to Deuteronomy 28:12 and 15:6, I lend to many nations but I shall not borrow.

+ According to Philippians 4:19, my God supplies all my need according to His riches in glory by Christ Jesus.

Health

+ According to 3 John 2, above all things I prosper, I am in heath even as my soul prospers.

+ According to Isaiah 53:5, by the stripes that Jesus took across His back I am healed.

+ According to Malachi 4:2, the sun of righteousness arose for me with healing in his wings and I am healed.

Family

+ According to Joshua 24:15, my house and I will serve the Lord.

+ According to Acts 16:31, my household and I are saved.

I want to encourage you to take every situation in your life and find a Scripture that covers that area. Then turn it into a confession spoken as if that verse is already done for you. As you speak your goals as confessions, and do the same with the Word, you will see monumental shifts in your life that will have an impact on everything in your world. I want you to know deep within that you have the power to shift your life, that you contain the very life giving words that are capsules to your future manifestations.

As you speak your goals as confessions, and do the same with the Word, you will see monumental shifts in your life that will have an impact on everything in your world.

When you use your divine right as a speaking spirit forged from the same material as your Creator, then you will see your circumstances change as you speak. You have the ability to speak a funeral or a blessing over your life. Why not speak what you want to see instead of what you are experiencing right now. Take a chance and discover what your words can do. They have the ability to cause heaven to intervene in your life. That's what prayer really is. It's when we allow heaven to converge in our everyday lives. Speaking faith-infused words is a form of prayer that will cause untold blessings. Speak what you want to be, not what you are now. Declare that your life will change and things will get better. Be unwavering in your resolve that you will have what you say and be exactly what God destined you to be. This is the true power of faith-filled confession.

PRINCIPLE SIX

6

PRINCIPLE SIX:
PLAN FOR IT

Now we have come to the final principle of the vision writing process. I think that this is a vital part of what we have done up to this point, and it may even be the most important phase. We have taken the time to write out our big dream in vision form. We have extracted the goals that give us a more concise version of the overall dream. Next, we took those goals and turned them into positive confessions that we can speak on a daily basis. The final part of this process is the plan. This is where we move from the visualizing and speaking to the actual doing.

PLANNING FOR SUCCESS

I have seen so many people instructed in the art of vision writing, goals, and positive confessions only to leave out the plan. It's in the plan that you take the first steps toward your dream. It's in the plan that you act on everything that's been turning within your spirit. It's the plan that activates and brings the unseen world to life. We are encouraged throughout Scripture to plan for our eventual success. Proverbs 16:3 says, *"Commit to the LORD whatever you do, and he will establish your plans"* (NIV). Your job, as discussed in the chapter 2, is to seek God for the vision He has for your life. Then all the plans you make from that point will be established by Him. What a plan does is draw a line from your vision to your manifestation. It's what you will do to ensure that the vision works, and it's also the steps you intend to take to get there.

> What a plan does is draw a line from your vision to your manifestation. It's what you will do to ensure that the vision works, and it's also the steps you intend to take to get there.

"May he give you the desire of your heart and make all your plans succeed" (Psalm 20:4 NIV). When you start working the principles of vision, you find that God's desire will become your desire. It's so important that you get in tune with your unique calling and gifts so that only your truest vision emerges.

I want you to repeat this to yourself: "God wants to give me my heart's desire." So many times, we are led to believe that God doesn't bless our efforts when, in all actuality, the opposite is true. God loves to see His children move forward into greater things.

"*No good thing will He withhold from them that walk uprightly*" (Psalm 84:11). God wants you to experience the best that life has to offer. He's not a withholding God; He is a God of blessing and an abundant life. God wants you to operate in your calling and experience the sheer bliss of following your purpose. The same thing is true about your plans. God promises us that He will make our plans succeed. Through the humble submission of yourself to the plan of God, you will gain access into His reservoir of unlimited favor and power. You will start to see things perfectly align for you as you plan for the success of your vision. In fact, that's the promise given here, that He will make all your plans succeed.

> **God wants to see you succeed. He didn't place you here to barely make it, to just get by, or to work yourself to death.**

I know that many of us were taught that God was a cruel and an indifferent entity. This thought may have solidified in our minds due to negative life experiences and difficulties we have faced. The greatest thing I can teach you, if nothing else, is that God wants to see you succeed. He didn't place you here to barely make it, to just get by, or to work yourself to death. No, the Lord placed you here to fulfill your destiny and enjoy the journey. It's my desire to teach you how to do this with your plan. I want to show how to take your vision and turn it into practical application.

You may be asking yourself, *What does a plan look like? How do I write one and what is its framework?* The plan-writing process is similar to the writing of your grand vision. You will have to use some faith and some practical thinking to formulate your plan. Let's take a look at how I did this using our examples from the last two chapters. The first thing we will do is write out our objective in the form of a mission statement, which explains your highest reason for doing what you are pursuing. Next we will write down three goals that support the accomplishment of our objective. Then we will write out three strategies that are the action steps to fulfilling our supporting goals for the overall objective.

MY PLAN FOR MINISTRY

Objective: I am reaching the world through my ministry by doing what I am called to do and helping people.

Goals:

1.   Preach in the International Holy Convocation.

2.   Be a guest on a Christian TV station.

3.   Be in full-time ministry.

Strategies:

1.   Send out clips of me preaching to all the bishops in my denomination/organization.

2.   Volunteer to guest on local TV shows that will lead to national TV shows.

3.   Volunteer at my local church.

You can see from the examples given that you are once again breaking down the larger entities of your vision and listing them in smaller parts. By doing this you get tangible action steps that you can begin working on. I want to stress here that writing a plan is the key to taking action on your dream. This principle gives you the "what to do" for what you have envisioned. As we will see, it's only when you take action that you will see your desires manifest.

ACTION LEADS TO ACTIVATION

Taking action is the difference between a weak prayer and having your heart's desire. Many times, what comes your way may seem trivial or small in comparison to what you have dreamed, but it's the small steps of your path that lead you to your destiny. You have to start somewhere and many times that starting place is at the bottom, but the bottom yields results that lead you to the top. I can think of so many times that this has proved true in my life.

If you recall from the first chapter, I described the scenario of me lying on the floor asking God what was wrong with me and why my life had come to such a dark place. After He revealed to me that I had lost my dream and that it was time to get it back, He gave me something to do. This something was no easy task for me.

I had been away from Birmingham for years. When I came back, few people knew that I was in town. While I was lying on that floor, God spoke to me and told me to call the pastor of my youth and ask him if I could volunteer at the church. You have to understand that I hadn't talked to him in years. Going all the way back to the place I had started was a humbling experience.

That's exactly what I did though. I called him and told him that I was back in town and that God was leading me to volunteer at his ministry. I told him that I didn't want anything from him but an opportunity to serve. I told him that I would do anything he wanted me to do. I would clean the toilets, mop the floors, or any other task that was needed. He asked me to come to his office and he would put me in the membership department. I was ecstatic for the opportunity. One of the duties of this position was to follow up with all the visitors who had filled out cards with their contact information. The first week I was there, I rounded up all the cards I could get my hands on. I comprised a stack of cards that hadn't been called in years. I went through each of those cards, prayed with people, and then invited them to join us for church. On one Sunday, I had over one hundred people show up for church as a result of the calls I was making. This type of action led me to a full-time paid position at the church.

The day I decided to do something and go back to my local church not only opened the door for me to earn a position, it also became the place where I came in contact with everyone that would assist me in reaching my ultimate goal of speaking at the convention.

During my tenure on staff at the church, I was put into the position of booking the speakers for our conferences. I had written in my vision that I would be exposed to three different people. The first was the marketing director for the Church of God in Christ. The second was the leader of the Pastors and Elders Council, and the third was the presiding Bishop. With all these people written into my vision, I had this internal understanding that somehow things would line up for me and I would meet these key figures that would be so instrumental in my future.

The first thing that happened was a service we had at our church, and the invited guest was the marketing director that I had written into my vision. When he arrived, I was able to go to lunch with him. We had an instant connection. A few months later, I was in his city and attended his church. He asked me to speak for him in at the evening service and I accepted. After that service he was so impressed with my ministry that he said he needed to give me some exposure to the church. I took this as a sign that my vision was working.

The next thing that happened tied in perfectly with that God moment. We were in our convocation at our local church and had the leader of the Elders Council speaking for us. This was, of course, the other person I had written about in my vision. I was sent to pick him up from the airport with an internal knowing that things were working again. When I met him at baggage claim, he was on the phone the entire time until we reached the car. While in the car, I overheard him telling the person on the other end where he was and about the church he was speaking at. The next thing that happened was so amazing and shows God's perfect synchronicity at work. He turned to me and asked, "Are you Shane Perry?" I told him I was. He then said, "I have someone who wants to speak with you." On the other line was the marketing director whom I had preached for only a month before! When I picked up the leader of the Elders Council for church that night, he told me that he had been informed that I was a great speaker and he wanted to use me soon. Sure enough it wasn't long before I was standing in front of a room full of pastors for the Church of God in Christ. This would be the next step in reaching my goal.

The next thing that transpired was having the presiding Bishop in town to speak for the last night of our convocation. Once again, I was assigned to pick him up from the airport. We had several preachers with us and we all went to lunch together. The next morning, he had to fly out early and we were scheduled again to have a number of preachers with us to see him off. This time, however, I was the only one to show up. Before I left the house early that morning, I grabbed a DVD of me speaking in one of the larger churches in the Church of God in Christ. I placed it in my suit jacket pocket and proceed to go meet the presiding Bishop. While we were on our way to the airport, he said to me, "I've heard that you are a really good speaker. Send a DVD to my office." I replied, "Bishop, I just so happen to have a DVD on me right now." I took out the DVD and he placed it in his bag. I knew that God was unfolding my vision right before my eyes. Two months after this encounter, I received a phone call asking if I would speak at the International Holy Convocation. My lifelong dream up to that point was secured!

The key to understanding how all this happened is found in my plan. I knew that I had to get around what I wanted to see happen in my life. Although I was completely broke and about to lose everything I owned, I made the choice to volunteer. That one act put me right where I needed to be to see my dream come to pass. I often say, "Submission puts you in position." It was in my ability to submit by going back to where it all started, trusting God with the process, and being willing to perform the most menial tasks that placed me where I ultimately needed to be.

As you work the plan for all of your goals, I want you to remember that you have to take action right where you are. There is always something you can immediately do to take steps toward your dream. It may be volunteering to help someone else reach their goals that ultimately leads you to your place of fulfillment. The key is that you have to *do something*. When you write out your plan, do it with this very thought in mind. Try doing this now for three of your goals.

MY PLAN FOR _____

Objective:

_____

_____

_____

_____

Goals:

_____

_____

_____

_____

Strategies:

_____

_____

_____

_____

MY PLAN FOR _____

Objective:

_____

_____

_____

_____

Goals:

_____

_____

_____

_____

_____

Strategies:

_____

_____

_____

_____

_____

MY PLAN FOR _____

Objective:

_____

_____

_____

_____

Goals:

_____

_____

_____

_____

Strategies:

_____

_____

_____

_____

FINAL THOUGHTS

7

FINAL THOUGHTS

Above all else I want you to know that regardless of the circumstances that got you here, you were created for a purpose. You will only know the satisfaction of a life well lived when you take a chance on your dream. Life is too short and too precious to squander it by working at a job you hate or spinning your wheels, stuck in the same place. If you're ready to live life as an adventure that unfolds into beauty, then you need only to heed the principles of this book. These principles are your ticket to liberation from the chains of the mundane and average. I know the type person you are. I know this because you picked up this book. Anyone who reads a book like this is someone looking for more out of life. As you follow these principles, you will see things miraculously showing up in your life that will lead and guide you into a better future.

You might still be thinking, *This is good and I'm glad it worked for you, but I'm not sure this will work for me.* Let me encourage you by saying I'm the least likely person to succeed in life. I was born the child of a rape in a poor family. I don't have an illustrious pedigree. I was set up to fall in line with all those who came before me. Yet, even as a child, I knew there was something out there that had to be bigger and better than what I saw around me. When I worked for the church in my earlier days, I knew that I was in training to make an even greater impact upon the world. When I was in the army, I would spend hours in the library reading and searching for a better way. It was only when I lay on the floor of my mother-in-law's house that I got the vision that would change my life.

I'm not special, I just have a clear-cut vision that I revise often, because things tend to manifest so rapidly. What I want to stress here is that if it worked for me it can work for you, too. The idea that one person is more special than another is erroneous. We all have the ability to tap into God's favor. Paul said, *"For there is no respect of persons with God"* (Romans 2:11). God does not regard one person over another. He offers the same ability to dream and access a better future to all. In fact, God is so abundant in His impartiality that Jesus said, *"For he gives his sunlight to both the evil and the good, and he sends the rain on the just and the unjust alike"* (Matthew 5:45 NLT). God so wants to bless His creation that He blesses *everyone*, regardless of their standing with Him. How much more will He open up His greatness to those that seek Him?

> **God does not regard one person over another. He offers the same ability to dream and access a better future to all.**

I want you to know that you can do this! You can be all that God has placed inside you to be. All you have to do is dream big and go for it. Will it be challenging at times? Of course, but with a written vision and the principles in this book, you will succeed in the end. Now is the time to set aside your fears. Make a decision that you will no longer listen to the voices of doubt. Step out of your comfort zone and dare to be different. We have been so trained to think like everyone else, to do things the way others do them, and to never challenge the status quo. Now is the time to start thinking independently of others and get a God-given vision for your future. I pray that you will be stimulated to dare to dream beyond where you are now. I pray that you will be so motivated by this book that you refuse to live another day below your God-given potential. You have a bright future waiting to unfold in magnificent ways if you will but dare to dream.

Make sure that you take the time at the end of this book to go back through each principle. Here's a quick review for your convenience:

- Write down in detail what you want your life to look like a year from now. Explain what your relationship with God and other people will look like. Explain what you would like to do for a living if you could do anything. Detail what type of house you would live in and where you would like this house to be. As you write, include the status of your health and the ideal weight that you would like to be. Remember, nothing off limits and you can dream as big as your imagination can take you.

+ Next, extract goals from the expansive vision that best capture the essence of what you have written. This is important because these goals give you clear targets to hit during your vision process.

+ Then, take these goals and turn them into positive confessions that you can speak in the now, as if you already have them. You should speak these confessions every day, preferably first thing in the morning and before bed. The reason these times are so important is because these are the two times that your mind is the most open to suggestion. Your brain waves go into lower frequencies when you awaken and before you go to sleep. These confessions form the basis from which you move to the next step.

+ The last principle is to take your goals and make plans. These plans are the actions that you will take that will bring manifestation to your dreams. In your plan, you should clearly state your objectives in the form of a mission statement. Then you will need three smaller, specific goals that support the ultimate goal. Finally, you need to write out the strategies for what you will do to take action on those goals.

It is my earnest desire that you will apply these principles to the areas of your life that you would like to change. So many times we think that change is a long process but, more often than not, it doesn't take as long as we thought. For me, major things changed in my life in just two years of following these principles. Even to this day, I follow a vision for my life and everything I have written down so far has eventually come to pass. I've seen doors open to me that may have seemed impossible to others. If they would only read the pages of this book they would know exactly how it all happened.

Everything has transpired in my life because I took a chance on doing something different and followed the Holy Spirit's guidance leading me toward my destiny. I want you to know that this joy of living life to the fullest can be yours too. I want you to know that you can and will become whatever you place your intention on. When you capture the vision in your spirit, allow it to invade your cerebral space, and make it what you say and do, nothing will be impossible for you. As you apply these principles, I leave you with the title of this book…*Dream It, Live It!* See it, be it, do it, and you'll get it. God bless you all in your endeavor to see yourself in the future and to live what you see.

ABOUT THE AUTHOR

ABOUT THE AUTHOR

Shane Perry Sr. is a man of focus, passion, and vision. He is a promoter of the gospel of Jesus Christ and the advancement of His kingdom on earth. He is known for his love of people and passion for ministry. He travels the world preaching a message of hope and teaching the masses how to find God's purpose for their life.

Shane Perry has an incredible approach and insight in his messages and teaches how to make them applicable in everyday life.

He has preached for some of the largest churches, conferences, corporate events, and television networks of our generation. He has graced the pulpit of Bishop T. D. Jakes of the Potters House Dallas, TX, as well as MegaFest, Bishop Jakes' largest conference. He has preached for Bishop Charles Edward Blake of West Angeles Church of God in Christ in Los Angeles, CA, Bishop Noel Jones at the City of Refuge Los Angeles, CA, and he has preached twice in the Holy Convocation of the Church of God in Christ both in Memphis and St. Louis, as well as many other churches and conferences around the world.

Shane Perry has hosted the international program *Praise the Lord* on Trinity Broadcasting Network (TBN) as well as been a frequent guest. He can also be seen on several other networks such as BET, TCT, Daystar, and INSP.

Additionally, Dr. Perry is a dedicated family man. He is happily married to Latoiya Perry. He has five children Arianna, Shane Jr., Autumn, Lauren, and Jaxon.

Welcome to Our House!

We Have a Special Gift for You

It is our privilege and pleasure to share in your love of Christian books. We are committed to bringing you authors and books that feed, challenge, and enrich your faith.

To show our appreciation, we invite you to sign up to receive a specially selected **Reader Appreciation Gift**, with our compliments. Just go to the Web address at the bottom of this page.

God bless you as you seek a deeper walk with Him!

WE HAVE A GIFT FOR YOU. VISIT:

whpub.me/nonfictionthx

WHITAKER
HOUSE